PRAISE FOR TH

Wow! What a needed resource for single men and women. Dating can be one of the most confusing times in a single person's life, and we desperately need solid biblical guidance in this area. Thank you, Sean and Spencer, for giving us this incredibly practical and biblical book on dating. We highly recommend it!

—**Kristen Clark and Bethany Baird**, Founders, GirlDefined Ministries; Coauthors, *Girl Defined: God's Radical Design for Beauty, Femininity, and Identity*

Sean and Spencer give terrific counsel on dating. Their words are wise, fired with passion, and biblically faithful. Those who are confused and even broken by our anything-goes era will find here a gospel-shaped path to ordered love—love as God ordains it.

—**Owen Strachan**, Associate Professor of Christian Theology, Midwestern Seminary; Coauthor, *The Grand Design: Male and Female He Made Them*

Authors and friends Sean Perron and Spencer Harmon have written a most helpful book on dating. Don't let the short chapters fool you—this book is packed with biblical wisdom for a journey on which we need it most. On a topic where some might veer into sentimentality, self-help, or legalism, Perron and Harmon strike a gracious and biblical tone throughout their work.

—**Jonathan Holmes**, Pastor of Counseling, Parkside Church, Uniontown, Ohio; Author, *The Company We Keep: In Search of Biblical Friendship*

Christian men and women who are seeking to understand how to make godly decisions concerning dating need to carefully study the wisdom of this book. Far too often, little thought is given to biblical direction concerning personal decisions about dating the opposite sex. Many think that since the Bible does not mention the idea of dating it is silent about the topic, but nothing is further from the truth. You will be surprised at the practical wisdom this book gives. We highly recommend it to you.

—**John D. and Janie L. Street**, Authors, *The Biblical Counseling Guide for Women*

If you want rock-solid biblical guidance on dating, read this book. If you want to think wisely and practically about how to handle a first date, parents, breaking up, pornography, kissing, past sexual history, or declining a date, read this book. If you want to honor Christ with your dating relationships, read this book. I can't wait to put *Letters to a Romantic: On Dating* into the hands of singles in my church!

—**Deepak Reju**, Pastor of Biblical Counseling and Family Ministry, Capitol Hill Baptist Church, Washington, DC; Author, *On Guard* and *The Pastor and Counseling*

Praise for Both *Letters to a Romantic* Books

Sean and Spencer are two old souls. They have a remarkable amount of wisdom to offer on these topics—wisdom well beyond their years. I wholeheartedly recommend anything these two godly men, exemplary husbands, and exceptional leaders have to say about how they met their wives, honored them from courtship into marriage, and now lead and love them in the way of Christ.

—**Dan DeWitt**, Director, Center for Biblical Apologetics and Public Christianity, Cedarville University; Author, *Jesus or Nothing* and *Christ or Chaos*

From romanticism, to breakups, to the issue of sexuality and singleness, Sean and Spencer provide us with a significant, biblical word for the areas of dating and engagement. No two areas are more ignored and yet more in need of a clear, concise word from God. These biblical counselors, with rare insight and discernment, lead you through the spiritual steps that will result in healthy, God-honoring, deepening relationships.

—**Mac and Debbie Brunson**, Cohosts of "The Fixer Upper Marriage" Bible Study, First Baptist Church, Jacksonville, Florida

Relationships require wisdom. God has given Sean and Spencer remarkable wisdom for their age. Their wisdom, seasoned with plenty of Scripture, written in the form of letters from a friend, is a recipe for real help for couples navigating dating and engagement.

—**C. J. Mahaney**, Senior Pastor, Sovereign Grace Church, Louisville, Kentucky

These books contain the kind of wise biblical advice an older brother or mentor would offer to a young person who is seeking to navigate the waters of romance and engagement. Their short-letter format makes them very easy (and fun) to read. Practical answers are given to the questions young people are most likely to raise.

—**Jim Newheiser**, Director of the Christian Counseling Program and Associate Professor of Practical Theology, Reformed Theological Seminary, Charlotte; Executive Director, Institute for Biblical Counseling and Discipleship

Letters to a Romantic: On Dating and *On Engagement* are wonderful guides written by two young men who have a lot of biblical wisdom. Each letter is engaging and very informative. In fact, they are so good that I have five young adults in mind to give them to. Perron and Harmon have done an exceptional job.

—**Martha Peace**, Biblical Counselor; Author, *The Excellent Wife* and *Damsels in Distress*

There's nothing easy about dating or getting engaged. I lurched through the process like most people—fearful, fumbling, and full of doubt. If only Sean and Spencer had written these books fifty years ago! But here they are just in time for you! Make a date with these books before booking a date. The Bible's advice is never dated for those who are engaged in its teachings.

—**Robert J. Morgan**, Teaching Pastor, The Donelson Fellowship, Nashville; Author, *The Strength You Need: The Twelve Great Strength Passages of the Bible*

In these two books on dating and engagement, Sean Perron and Spencer Harmon have given us a treasure trove of biblically based practical information for all unmarried Christians. I am very grateful to God for giving Sean and Spencer the desire and ability to write these two books. They contain information that I wish had been available for me to give to Christians as they thought about dating or engagement. I will certainly have them at the ready to give to Christians who need biblically based answers to the plethora of relevant issues that godly people who are thinkers will have about these topics.

    —**Wayne Mack**, Director and Professor, Strengthening Ministries Training Institute; Director, Association of Certified Biblical Counselors—Africa

Sean Perron and Spencer Harmon are full of wise, gospel-centered counsel on navigating through singleness, dating, and engagement. Whatever your season of life, you will find yourself better equipped to guide others and to strengthen your own faith by reading these books.

    —**Russell Moore**, President, Ethics & Religious Liberty Commission of the Southern Baptist Convention

letters
TO A
Romantic

Letters

TO A

Romantic

ON DATING

SEAN PERRON
& SPENCER HARMON

P&R

PUBLISHING

P.O. BOX 817 • PHILLIPSBURG • NEW JERSEY 08865-0817

Italics within Scripture quotations indicate emphasis added.

Printed in the United States of America

Library of Congress Cataloging-in-Publication Data

Names: Perron, Sean, author.
Title: Letters to a romantic : on dating / Sean Perron, Spencer Harmon.
Description: Phillipsburg : P&R Publishing, 2017.
Identifiers: LCCN 2017029922| ISBN 9781629953045 (pbk.) | ISBN 9781629953052 (epub) | ISBN 9781629953069 (mobi)
Subjects: LCSH: Single people--Conduct of life. | Dating (Social customs)--Religious aspects--Christianity. | Marriage--Religious aspects--Christianity.
Classification: LCC BV4596.S5 P47 2017 | DDC 241/.6765--dc23
LC record available at https://lccn.loc.gov/2017029922

To Jenny:

The world is not worthy of you,
and neither am I.

—Sean

To Taylor:

The most faith-filled, loyal, and
trustworthy person I know. I love you.

—Spencer

CONTENTS

FOREWORD

If you are currently reading this book, you are most likely in one of the most uncomfortable relationships possible. This complicated and awkward time of life begins just before a young man and woman start to date and ends when that same couple gets engaged. This was true in my own personal experience as a young man, and I know it now as a pastor, having walked through this clumsy season with dozens of young couples—including the men who authored this book when they were in that season themselves.

Think about how uncomfortable this time of life can be. A guy notices a girl and finds her attractive, godly, funny, interesting, and normal. He is very interested in her. Then there's the girl. She notices the guy. She thinks he's godly, handsome, funny, interesting, and less socially awkward than most guys she's been around. She is very interested in him. But how should they move forward from there? Neither has any real way of knowing if the other person has the same level of interest. So the agonizing commences: nervousness permeates, the pressure weighs down, and friends get involved—with varying degrees of wisdom. And this is in ideal circumstances! Things only get more complicated when only one person is interested in romance, when there are varying degrees of parental preference regarding the relationship, when friends disagree over whether the relationship is a good idea, and when there is disagreement on how the relationship should be defined (is this dating, courting, talking, pursuing a closer relationship, seeing each other, or just getting to know each other a bit better?). The whole thing is maddening.

Then, every once in a while and against all odds, you catch lightning in a bottle and spend time together. But now the problems multiply. How are you to know whether the other person likes you as much as you like them? Should you hold hands? Hug? Kiss? What about how much time you spend together? How much is too much? If you're not together enough, your girlfriend (is she okay with you calling her that?) might think that you don't like her. If you're around her too much, she'll think you're a stalker. How do you know when it is appropriate to communicate your deepest feelings to this person?

Dating relationships are complicated because they come at the intersection of four realities: sin, inexperience, high stakes, and a lack of familiarity. Sin is involved because—more than we care to admit—sinful desires lie behind our decisions, motivating us to pursue relationships for all sorts of wrong reasons, including sinful sexual motivations, the desire to date someone who will raise our social status or who we believe is good looking enough for us, and countless other bad reasons. We also deal with the limitation of inexperience. Let's be honest—how much can we be expected to know about such crucial matters when we've been alive for only twenty years or so and thus legal adults for only two? The stakes are also high. Most of us understand that a dating relationship could very easily become a marriage relationship, and we do not want to mess up something so crucial. Finally, we lack familiarity with the other person. It takes time to get to know someone well, but in this case we are making important decisions based on a relationship only a few days or weeks old.

To get beyond these problems we need wisdom. That is why I am so thrilled about this book, for it is written by two men whom God has graced with great wisdom. Sean Perron and Spencer Harmon are two of my favorite men in the world. I have known them for years as a professor, boss, pastor, and friend and have walked with them through their respective dating relationships, engagements, and marriages (I have great stories that you should ask me about sometime!). I have seen these men receive God's grace as they walked through their own dating relationships, and I have seen them communicate this wisdom to others. I'm glad that they can share their wisdom with you in the pages of this book. You need to learn from what God has shown these guys.

As I write these words, I can hear my wife, Lauren, downstairs. Almost fifteen years ago I began to pursue her (that is what we decided to call it back then). By our second date, about eight days after we had become "official," I knew that I wanted to marry her. I had never felt that way before, and I wasn't sure what to do with the desire. I decided (wisely) to withhold communicating this until a later time. As I always tell people, our dating relationship involved me waiting for the right time to tell her what I knew I wanted to say two weeks after we started dating. There were days and weeks of struggle in that waiting. There were times when I was sure I was more interested in her than she was in me. I wondered if our relationship would survive when I moved away to seminary. For a time I even wondered whether her parents would allow her to marry a guy who they knew would move her away. But we made it.

As of last month she has had my last name for thirteen years.

As I've listened to her downstairs for the last few minutes, I have heard her singing "Crown Him with Many Crowns," laughing with our kids, calling our dog into the house, and correcting one of our sons who was sinning against our daughter. When our journey together began, a decade and a half ago, I had no idea that it would produce this much joy. But God was kind. I want you to know that he will be kind to you as well.

Trust God to give you his wisdom. And then pray for it— God promises to give wisdom when we request it in faith (see James 1:5). Then turn the page and begin reading *Letters to a Romantic: On Dating*. You will find that, as you do, God will begin to answer your prayer.

Heath Lambert
Jacksonville, FL
August 2016

INTRODUCTION

HOW TO THINK ABOUT
DATING (AND THIS BOOK)

Sean and Spencer

Dear Reader,

You are about to read a collection of letters covering a wide range of topics related to dating and romance. We have written these letters to you because we are convinced that God cares about you and your relationships. These letters are not designed to argue a particular dating method or give a play-by-play of "courtship." Instead, our goal is to demonstrate how the Bible gives meaningful and practical advice when it comes to pursuing romance.

We are convinced that our God is a worthy God. We believe that Jesus deserves all the glory that this world can possibly produce. This means that Jesus wants you to bring him honor and fame in every possible scenario you may encounter in your romantic relationships. We are also convinced that people are happiest when they seek to bring Jesus glory and that they were created to experience the joy of living for the majesty of God.[1] The foundation for our book can be narrowed down to three truths:

1. God deserves glory from everything—including romance (see Col. 1:16).
2. We experience true happiness when we seek to glorify God in everything—including romance (see 1 Cor. 10:31).
3. In the Bible, God tells everything we need to know to enable us to bring him glory and us joy—and this includes our romance (2 Peter 1:3).

We are not relational gurus. Quite the opposite—we would be the first to admit to you that when we follow our own wisdom we get lost. We are sinners desperately in need of God's illuminating Word in every facet of our lives. We have made mistakes, we have regrets, and we need wisdom and grace from God and others. Yet, despite our shortcomings, we have come to see that the Bible has essential, important, and practical things to say about romance.

The letters you will read are arranged so that they build on each other, but they can be read in any order. Each chapter is designed to be short and practical but not comprehensive. Even though we don't know the specifics of your situation, we have made a concerted effort to make the chapters as relevant as possible. It is our prayer that this content will be immediately helpful and tangible rather than overly narrow or rigid.

---

1. Our thoughts have been shaped and influenced by John Piper's book *Desiring God: Meditations of a Christian Hedonist*, rev. ed. (Colorado Springs: Multnomah, 2011). For further reading on this topic, check out Piper's short book *The Dangerous Duty of Delight: Daring to Make God Your Greatest Desire* (Sisters, OR: Multnomah, 2001).

Our wives, Jenny Perron and Taylor Harmon, have also contributed to many of the letters and have provided their own warm touches throughout.

Use this book in whichever way best serves you and your relationship. Skip around, read it alone, or go through it as a couple or with a group of friends. There are questions at the end of each chapter to help you think through the content in a personal way. The point of this book is to start a conversation, not to have the whole conversation for you. Also, before you dive into this book, it might be helpful to identify several older, more mature Christians who can talk through these issues with you.

Whether you are struggling with singleness, enduring a breakup, beginning a new relationship, or making the final step toward engagement, we believe it is the pursuit of Christ *through his Word* that will allow you to address *any* dating issue with confidence. We have prayed this for you and hope that you will see and cherish this theme as you read.

Until then,
Sean and Spencer

MARRIAGE VS. SINGLENESS

Sean and Jenny

Dear Romantic,

Romance is a wonderful gift from God. Rightly understood, it is full of passion, commitment, risk, and adventure. It is an incredible journey that originates with God. From the very beginning, God designed everyone to be in love with him. He longs for this so intensely that, while we were still sinners, God sent his son Jesus to die for us (see Rom. 5:8). God took on human flesh and suffered the excruciating pain of the cross so that the world could have a relationship with him (see John 3:16).

God desires everyone to know and become addicted to his steadfast love (see Psalm 63:3). This divine romance is available for everyone who believes in Jesus Christ and receives forgiveness for sin. Yet, while God wants everyone to experience his love, he doesn't want everyone to fall in love with another person. Some will fall in love and get married, but the Bible teaches that some will not.

The apostle Paul encourages people, in 1 Corinthians 7, to

remain single for the sake of the gospel. Singleness is actually *best*, according to Paul. He commends singleness because of the benefits it holds for the kingdom of God. "The unmarried man is anxious about the things of the Lord, how to please the Lord. But the married man is anxious about worldly things, how to please his wife, and his interests are divided" (1 Cor. 7:32–34). There are some people who are so captivated by the romance of God that they intend to stay single for life. Marriage is a distraction to them. But how can you tell whether you should or should not stay single for life?

Marriage and singleness each have their own unique ways of displaying the life, death, and resurrection of Jesus. In fact, the Bible describes both singleness and marriage as gifts from God.

Notice these gifts in 1 Corinthians 7:6–7:

> Now as a concession, not a command, I say this. I wish that all were as I myself am. But each has *his own gift* from God, one of one kind and one of another.

A gift is a good thing. James says that every good and perfect gift comes down from above from the Father of lights (see James 1:17). God never gives bad gifts to his children. Every Christian contemplating whether or not to pursue an earthly romance should ask, "Do I have the gift of singleness or the gift of marriage?"

HOW TO KNOW IF YOU HAVE THE GIFT OF SINGLENESS

Paul answers this question in 1 Corinthians 7:9: "But if they cannot exercise self-control, they should marry. For it is better to marry than to burn with passion." If you have the gift of singleness, you won't be continually burning with passion for a spouse. You are pleased without parenthood and satisfied without sex. Your mind is currently occupied with the work of the gospel, and the desire for sex rarely crosses your mind. If this describes you, you likely have the gift of singleness, even if just for this season of life.

Here is one example that may help you as you think through this issue. Jenny and I had a close friend who served with me in our church. He was always one of the first church members to volunteer whenever a need arose. One day it dawned on me that I had never heard him express romantic interest in a girl. He was in his late twenties and was a godly man, a true gentleman. The majority of his friends were in dating relationships or were newly married.

So I asked him whether he was interested in pursuing anyone for marriage. He confessed that he didn't spend time thinking about marriage or dating. He was not consumed with lust, and rarely did he think about sex unless someone else brought up the topic. He wasn't interested in any girls romantically, preferring instead to spend this season of his life investing in his local church.

Nothing was wrong with him. Nothing needed to be fixed. He didn't obsess over whether or not he was missing out on God's will for his life. He wasn't introspective or consumed with whether he had the gift of singleness or marriage. He was simply passionate about serving his church—not burning with passion for a spouse. He had the gift of singleness.

If you have the gift of singleness, seize it for the glory of God. Take life by the horns, risks and all. Launch into the fray of ministry with abandonment. Invest in others without restriction or reservation. The single person doesn't have to worry about buying a one-way ticket to the nations to spread the good news of Jesus. Single people can serve faithfully in their churches, welcome people into their homes, visit orphans, feed the hungry, excel in their workplaces, and share the gospel.

HOW TO KNOW IF YOU HAVE
THE GIFT OF MARRIAGE

But what if you do desire a spouse? What if you long to have a family and to love someone exclusively without reserve? This might mean that marriage is for you.

On the surface, singleness may look more holy, but marriage is not for those who are unable to board the radical boat or are left behind on the unspiritual dock. Marriage is not for the less godly or for those with less gusto for the gospel. No, marriage is also for those who are zealous about God.

God designed marriage to display his glory in a unique way. If you have the gift of marriage, don't bail because you feel less spiritual. Marriage involves taking someone by the hand and serving with that person until the very end. It means taking up a job, having kids, loving others wholeheartedly, adopting the orphan, feeding your neighbor, showing hospitality, serving in your church, working hard for your employer, and telling others about Christ.

Once you figure out what gift you have, work toward using it. If you know that you want to pursue marriage in the future, go ahead and take steps toward that end. For instance, instead of backpacking across Europe, take a cooking class or develop your skills in a trade. Learn to provide for your future household.

Whatever you do, don't buy the lie of "Twenty Things You Have to Do in Your Twenties before Marriage." Blog posts like these are everywhere, and they treat marriage like a killjoy. Don't be duped into thinking that you have to "live it up before you settle down." Marriage isn't a drag. There is nothing wrong with a bucket list, but don't waste your life by making everything about you. And if you really want to take that backpacking trip, who says you can't do it with your spouse?

"He who finds a wife finds a good thing" (Prov. 18:22). At the same time, he who chooses the single life lives well. The point of 1 Corinthians 7 is to be faithful to what you are called. Live each season putting God first in your heart. Advance the kingdom of Jesus according to the desires God has given you and the circumstances he has placed you in—even if they are not what you expected. If your heart longs for a spouse and the Lord provides one, it is no sin to marry. Receive that gift; do not reject it.

> For everything created by God is good, and nothing is to be rejected if it is received with thanksgiving, for it is made holy by the word of God and prayer. (1 Timothy 4:4–5)

Whether your gift is singleness or marriage, purpose now to love the Lord with all your heart, soul, mind, and strength (see Mark 12:30). Lose yourself in this divine romance.

Until then,
Sean and Jenny

DISCUSSION QUESTIONS

1. Do you believe that you have the gift of singleness or the gift of marriage?
2. Do trusted friends and church members believe that you have the gift of singleness or of marriage? Have you asked them?

3. How often does the desire for marriage and sex cross your mind?
4. Does seeing others begin a relationship make you long for one too? If so, why?
5. What is one practical way you can begin cultivating your gift in order to serve others?

PREPARING FOR ROMANCE

Spencer

Dear Romantic,

The Bible says it best: "It is not good that the man should be alone" (Gen. 2:18).

I've always said "Yes and amen" to this verse. It goes on to say that God made "a helper fit for him." This also always received my hearty "Yes and amen." But it was the in-between phase—the phase when I was trying to figure out who I wanted to be with—that made me uneasy: restlessness brought by yearning for a companion, self-inflicted duress fueled by the advice of older married peers, the sheer thought of one day deciding that *this person* is *the person* (and knowing that *for sure*).

For me, the tension was in maintaining a balance. How could I balance physical attraction and inward beauty? How could I balance finding someone who was different enough to complement me while also ensuring that we were compatible? How could I balance encouragement from couples I respected, and advice from others, without being controlled by them? How could I know *for sure*?

To add to the confusion, the Bible doesn't give detailed instructions on how to navigate every nuance of dating. The Scriptures are sufficient to guide you, but the Bible does not work like a GPS on your phone when it comes to dating. Instead, it gives us *categories* that we must deeply consider and then apply to our lives. God has given us as Christians categories through which we can process our most complex issues—including the issue of whether or not we should pursue, date, and marry someone. Thankfully, God has promised that the Word will be a lamp to our feet and a light to our path (see Ps. 119:105).

Your stomach might be churning as you consider pursuing a relationship (or continuing in your current relationship). You know that pursuing a relationship can lead to marriage, and you know how serious marriage is. The commitment makes your head spin. What was an exhilarating adventure of learning about someone else has become a tangled knot of responsibility and decision making. Now you are trying to decide whether to run *toward* or *away from* romance. Or maybe your stomach is not churning at all, nor are you concerned about running from romance. You think that pursuing a relationship is like coasting with no direction. But you need to get serious; you need to decide which direction to run or at least to begin running. So, as you consider whether or not you should pursue a relationship, consider these three categories.

1. WHAT IS MY FOUNDATION? FEAR VS. FAITH

Faith is the beating heart of the Christian. By it we are brought into the family of God (see Rom. 3:28), and without it we cannot please God (see Heb. 11:6). It is the posture of the heart that has been made right with God and the lifeblood that animates our lives.

God loves faith, and throughout our lives he is always putting us in situations where it must be exercised. Prayer, suffering, and persecution are just a few areas in which God calls his people to practice faith. When we bleed faith in a difficult circumstance, we show the world that God is a rock worthy of building our lives upon (see 1 Peter 3:14–16).

As you prepare for romance, look down at your feet and examine whether you stand on the rock of faith or the sand of fear. Remember that fear or faith can motivate you toward or away from a relationship. You may know that you should not continue in a relationship right now, but you won't end it because you are afraid of being alone. But, instead of fearing, God calls you to wait *by faith*—trusting that he will tend to your cares and provide what you need in his time (see 1 Peter 5:6–8; Phil. 4:19). Or you may be ready to pursue a relationship but are paralyzed by the fear of commitment and the unknown terrain of dating, engagement, and marriage. Instead of fearing the unknown, however, God calls you toward pursuing a relationship *by faith*—trusting that his presence with you through the unknown will sustain you (see Isa. 41:10).

Fear can kill our relationships. We will never experience full and lasting relationships if they are in the death grip of fear. The God who knows all things and orchestrates them for the good of his people is calling you to build (or perhaps to postpone) your relationship through faith in his goodness.

2. WHAT IS MY VISION? MAN'S WORLD VS. GOD'S WORD

As a citizen of heaven, you are a pilgrim traveling through this world (see Phil. 3:20). Later on we will discuss some of the obvious dangers to avoid in the world, such as impurity, idolatry, and the neglect of community. These are the sins that derail and end relationships.

But before we discuss the pitfalls along the road, we must ensure that we are reading the right map. The temptation for many of us is far subtler than explicit sin: we let our *vision* of dating and relationships be informed by man's world rather than God's Word. This is significant because our *vision* of dating creates our *expectations* for dating. If our expectations are informed by a world that is in rebellion against God (see 1 John 5:19), then our relationships will be stained with upside-down values that prioritize short-term, second-rate things that will leave us bitter, disappointed, and impossible to please. We need a better map to guide us on this journey.

As you consider whether or not you should pursue or continue in a relationship, ask yourself this question: Are my thoughts and concerns about romance and relationships informed and motivated by God's Word or by man's world? Perhaps you value the way that her body looks more than you value the inward person of her heart (see Prov. 31:30). Perhaps you care more about his charisma than his character (1 Peter 3:7). Perhaps you think more about pleasing the person in front of you than about the Person who is always with you (Isa. 2:22). These disproportionate values are worldly and opposed to God's Word. Is your mind being transformed *away from* these values or conformed *toward* these values? Evaluate your expectations under the microscope of God's Word—what do you find?

The most radical thing you can do for your future relationship is to prioritize the fruits of the Spirit, which are found in God's Word (see Gal. 5:22–23). Consider which fruit your heart is cultivating before you move forward.

3. WHAT ARE MY EXPECTATIONS? COMPARISON VS. CONTENTMENT

Comparison is poison that will eventually affect every aspect of your relationships. This poison will infuse any potential romantic relationship with unrealistic expectations about your partner and will cloud your thinking from seeing them for who they really are. Comparison sets a utopian expectation for relationships that God never promised in a fallen world and compels us to run when we should stay.

The problem with comparison is that it never has enough. Even if you were to end a relationship because you believe there may be something better, you won't find it. Seeking to find heaven within a spouse is like trying to find the ocean in a stream, the city in a signpost.[1]

Comparison ultimately dishonors God by limiting his creativity to your own box of preferences. God's purpose for your future spouse, whoever that person may be, is unique and is not meant to be limited by our sinful expectations. Our expectations must be expanded by a breath of God's fresh air from Scripture. Experience God's creative pleasure by letting contentment inform your relationships. God intends for you to experience joy in your future spouse through your *differences* and to be sanctified by living with another person in an understanding way (see 1 Peter 3:7). But you will experience those differences only by growing in your contentment with who God made others to be, not by giving God advice about who your future spouse should be.

1. This idea is inspired by C. S. Lewis, *Surprised by Joy* (1955; repr., London: HarperCollins, 2012), 276–77, and C. S. Lewis, *The Weight of Glory* (1949; repr., New York: HarperCollins, 2001), 25–46.

GROWTH THROUGH THE CHURNING

Believe it or not, the churning in your stomach is a vehicle of growth. God means to grow you through various types of trials (see James 1:2–4) and by having you follow him in faith even when you don't feel like it (see James 1:25). Check your foundation, adjust your vision, inform your expectations, and make your move in faith. And know that God promises his presence with you through this decision—and through every decision to come.

Until then,
Spencer

DISCUSSION QUESTIONS

1. Describe your expectations for romance. Where do they come from?
2. How does fear manifest itself in your relationship?
3. In what ways does your perspective on romance need to change in light of God's Word?

SORROW AND JOY
IN SINGLENESS

Spencer

Dear Romantic,

Let's be honest: marriage celebrations aren't always joyful.

Of course, plenty of people at weddings are overflowing with joy: the older couple reminiscing on their own wedding joy, the newly engaged couple dreaming of their own wedding day, the parents of the bride and groom beaming with pride. But marriage celebrations can also be painful reminders of a persistent suffering—the suffering of singleness. To be sure, there are single people who are *not* suffering. They are content with their season of life, enjoying the freedom that singleness brings. For others, however, singleness is a burden that they struggle to carry. They long for the companionship of a spouse, coming home to a friend, and the intimacy of love.

You may know exactly what I'm talking about. You enjoy weddings, engagement parties, and the excitement of matrimony. Yet there is a tinge of pain—perhaps felt on the drive home or as you hear another couple make their vows—that reverberates in your heart. You long to rejoice with your friends, but you struggle with this unmet desire.

On top of this, you hear the call of the Bible to rejoice with those who rejoice, but your heart does not *feel it*. How are you supposed to rejoice while suffering? Can this sorrow and joy exist within the same heart?

THE COMPOSITE JOY OF THE BODY OF CHRIST

If we are honest, many of us hear the call to "rejoice with those who rejoice" (Rom. 12:15) as a mandate to produce a forced smile at an engagement party. We think, "Good for them," and may genuinely mean it. However, the dominant tone of our hearts is a deep groan of "How long, O Lord?"

But rejoicing with those who rejoice is not like forcing a smile for a family photo. It is the *ownership of another's joy because you see God at work*. The joy you are called to experience at your friend's engagement party or marriage ceremony is not some blind naiveté that ignores your own desires to be married. Instead, it is the celebration of God's good plans in the life of someone who is deeply connected to you.

This means that your joy is meant to be a composite joy. The joy of the Christian is equally composed of the work of God in one's own life and the work of God in the lives of fellow Christians. This is what Paul means when he writes, "If one member suffers, all suffer together; if one member is honored, all rejoice together" (1 Cor. 12:26). The joy of the Christian is a tapestry that interweaves the threads of our lives with the lives of others.

So the engagement party or marriage ceremony of your friend is actually an opportunity for you to experience *real, warm-hearted joy*. When we find it difficult to celebrate with another Christian, typically it is not because we are incapable of doing so. Rather, it's because we are not *willing* to experience joy in this way. We limit the potential moments of rejoicing in our lives to those times when things align to our preferences. The world transforms into a small, clenched fist that holds our plans, rather than the big world in which our happy God is busy blessing his children (see Jer. 32:41).

How do you view other believers and their joy? Do they become only catalysts of despair anytime they get something that *you* don't have? Or are they instead members of the same body as you, so that their joy is your joy? Are you soaking yourself in the reality that the church is the body of Christ—your family—so that the metaphor becomes truth? The key to rejoicing with those who rejoice is to see the victories of others as your own.

JOY AND SORROW UNDER THE SAME ROOF

But most singles are not dominated only by despair at an engagement party or marriage ceremony. Instead, we often experience a tangled web of joy and sorrow, pleasure and frustration, contentment and restlessness. We rejoice to see God at work, but our desire for marriage aches like a tender bruise. This isn't selfishness—it's a reminder of unwanted suffering.

Singles often experience unnecessary guilt because they don't understand the idea of *earnest waiting*. Earnest waiting happens when the truths of God's sovereignty and our responsibility meet in the suffering of our lives. When we as Christians suffer, two responses should arise from our hearts. First, we are called to *wait on the Lord*. The posture of our hearts is to be that of a weaned child trusting its parent (see Ps. 131:2). We are not to take matters into our own hands but instead are to hope fully in our God (see Ps. 37:34; 62:5; Prov. 20:22). For many Christian singles, this is the primary battleground. However, Christians are also called to *be persistent with the Lord.* A wrong application of the sovereignty of God is to assume that we are not to pray for relief from suffering. Although the heroes of our faith trusted God, Hannah prayed for a child (see 1 Sam. 1:9–18), the church in Acts prayed for Peter to be released from prison (see Acts 12:5), and Jesus honors persistence (see Luke 18:1–8).

It is not sinful to feel the sting of unwanted singleness at a marriage ceremony. It is sinful to allow this sting to translate into a heart that grumbles against the Lord and others. You can be sorrowful and joyful at the same time, but you cannot *grumble* and rejoice at the same time. Do your sorrows roll up into prayer toward the God who knows your needs? Or do your sorrows knot up your soul with complaining?

SORROWFUL, YET ALWAYS REJOICING

The pendulum could be swinging either way for you right now. You may be sorrowful, joyful, or maybe a mixture of both. Either way, God calls you to take steps of faith *now.* Are you sorrowful? Call on friends to partner with you as you pray for a spouse and for patience as you wait on the Lord. Are you joyful? Cultivate a lifestyle that loses itself in the joy of others. Go all out to celebrate the work of God in the lives of others by attending parties, serving at weddings, and giving your life away for the good of others. In other words, *live the Christian life*—weeping and laughing, repenting and believing, grateful while groaning.

These truths are not to be applied exclusively to singleness and marriage. The Christian life is full of trials, and yet we are called to rejoice in those trials (see 1 Peter 4:12–13). We are not asked merely to rejoice with those who rejoice; we are called to rejoice *in God* (see Hab. 3:18; Phil. 4:4). This rejoicing in God is the bedrock for sharing joy with others. In singleness—and in a million other sufferings—our hearts must be confident that he does not withhold good things from those who walk uprightly (see Ps. 84:11).

Until then,
Spencer

DISCUSSION QUESTIONS

1. When is it most difficult for you to rejoice with others? Why?
2. Do you think singleness can be a form of suffering? Why or why not?
3. Is it harder for you to persist in prayer or to wait on the Lord?

CONTENTMENT IN DATING

Sean and Jenny

Dear Romantic,

Too many singles pass their days wishing they were married. Single girls dream of their wedding day by pinning pictures on their Pinterest boards—just in case they happen upon a relationship tomorrow. Bachelors twiddle their thumbs while mentally designing the ideal timeline for their next potential candidate. Whether it's hanging paper lights on a virtual altar or calculating the perfect proposal for the mystery Mrs., something is missing.

THE CYCLE OF DISCONTENTMENT

Oddly enough, even dating couples sometimes believe the false idea that the season they are experiencing is actually a session in purgatory. Instead of enjoying each phase of their relationship and using it to grow in godliness, many people waste portions of their lives because they view them as hindrances. Dating and engagement are often treated as necessary obstacles to marriage.

Jenny and I can't help but notice that discontentment gives some couples a low-grade fever that is contagious. The irony thickens because married people can be just as restless in their dreams. We once heard a married friend confess that he wished he was single in order to have more time to read, study, serve, and spend for the kingdom. Yet the greatest irony is that this friend was likely just as disgruntled when he was single!

Notice the inevitable cycle: discontent singles become discontent marrieds. The seasons of dating and engagement are just canals in between.

The problem is not our season of life, our marriage status, or any of our circumstances. The issue is the contentment of our hearts. There are many discontent relationships that become discontent marriages, and I don't want yours to be one of them. The good news is that there is a solution. The apostle Paul wrote,

> I have learned in whatever situation I am to be content. I know how to be brought low, and I know how to abound. In any and every circumstance, I have learned the secret of facing plenty and hunger, abundance and need. I can do all things through him who strengthens me. (Phil. 4:11–13)

Listen carefully to three things that Paul mentions.

EVERY CIRCUMSTANCE

First, no situation could sway Paul's satisfaction, because Christ was sufficient. In "whatever situation" or "every circumstance," he wasn't disgruntled.

This includes the best of times and the worst of times. Whether you were dumped last Friday, are currently sky-high on the thought of dating and engagement, or are cherishing the thrills of marriage, you need contentment. Contentment in Christ needs to make its way into every crevice of your every circumstance.

THE FULLNESS OF CHRIST

Second, Paul was fulfilled because he was fastened to the fullness of Christ. His heart was firm, trusting in the Lord (see Ps. 112:7). Is Jesus enough, or do you need marriage in order to be complete? If you were to die before you said your vows, would this segment of your life have gone to waste (see Heb. 9:27)? Do you grumble and complain about your current season of life (see Phil. 2:14)?

I'm not trying to talk you out of pursuing marriage. It is more than possible to be satisfied with Christ alone while also having a good desire for marriage. My goal is for you to live each season to the fullest.

Strong desires in this season are not wrong. For example, it's good to have a desire for sex within the confines of marriage, but it all depends on what you do with that desire. A godly couple will pursue self-controlled minds that desire only to experience sexual intimacy in marriage for the glory of Christ. An immature couple will blaze with lustful fantasies that are full of impatience and disregard.

Or perhaps you continually get caught in the trap of comparison. You are always wishing your partner had a quality that you see in someone else. Now is the time to take these thoughts captive and kill any habit of comparison. As believers, we can take sinful thoughts and replace them with thankful thoughts controlled by the Spirit. Contentment can be found in the fruit of the Spirit, which includes love, joy, peace, patience . . . and *self-control.*

STRENGTH TO BE SATISFIED

Third, contentment is attainable for the Christian. The secret to Paul's satisfaction has to do with Christ, who "strengthens" him. Jesus is near to you and able to help you with this issue. This is what Paul is getting at in Philippians 4:11–13. Not only is Christ enough, but he also provides the strength for us to believe he is enough. Paul was able to do *all* things—including being content—through Christ. You and I have the same Christ who makes this possible.

Did you notice that Paul says he "learned" the secret of contentment? Learning takes time and effort. Don't envision contentment as a bright light that automatically comes on when you enter your house. Contentment is a fireplace, not a light switch. Think of contentment like a fire in your hearth that starts small but eventually warms your entire home and gives it a beautiful glow.

If your heart is restless instead of content, start digging your roots down deep in the waters of the Word. Become like a tree planted by streams of water that bears fruit in its season (see Ps. 1:3). Draw near to God by reading his Word in faith, praying to him, having conversations about him, and serving as he commands, and he will draw near to you. Resist the Devil and he will flee from you (see James 4:7–9). Believe that in Christ you have everything you need to glorify God and enjoy him forever. Whether you can hear the ringing of wedding bells in your future or you remain single for the rest of your days, ask the Lord for strength to be content in him. Write out specific thoughts that trouble you and memorize short statements of Scripture to replace them.

The happiest people in life are not marked by either singleness or marriage but by seizing each season for the glory of God.

This relationship *with him* is the one that you want. The grass is greenest where we gaze upon God. There is a time for everything, and every time is for God (see Eccl. 3; 12:13). May you enjoy each season to the highest by enjoying God to the fullest.

Until then,
Sean and Jenny

DISCUSSION QUESTIONS

1. If you are struggling with being content, write out the following passages to replace those sinful thoughts that creep into your mind: Psalm 121, Psalm 131, and Philippians 4:11–13.
2. List three people you can serve during this season in order to shift your focus toward others.
3. What are three practical ways you can serve those three people?

SHOULD I DATE A
NON-CHRISTIAN?

Sean

Dear Romantic,

Is it okay to date a non-Christian? Perhaps you are romantically interested in an unbeliever or, for one reason or another, have found yourself in a relationship with a non-Christian. It is very possible to imagine an unbeliever who is hard to resist. All the right factors could be in place—cute charm, dreamy looks, social suave, and a pleasant appeal. The only thing missing is . . . Jesus.

It might even appear that the non-Christian doesn't necessarily oppose Jesus. She doesn't show an outward hostility toward God, the Bible, church, or even moral living. It just isn't something she talks about much or "gets into."

Perhaps dating a Christian is just what such a person needs. He may be so close to the truth and may love so many good things that the Bible supports. It is not completely irrational for you to think that he would be compelled to follow Christ fully if he were enticed by a godly companion. Any compassion or desire for him to be saved is worthy of praise and should not be quenched.

You may want to reach out with the gospel (and this is the right instinct and action), but I am not convinced that romance is the way to go about evangelizing. I don't think the way to share Christ is through candlelit dinners and gushy love notes. The way of the Great Commission isn't "flirt to convert." I believe there is a better way to both display the love of Christ and protect your soul.

TRUE LOVE IS SOUL DEEP

It would be good to ask yourself this question: what do you find romantically attractive in someone who is not a believer? It would be unbiblical and frankly ridiculous for me to say that all unbelievers are repulsive. Every human is made in the image of God and bears his beautiful thumbprint. Unbelievers can be kind, generous, endearing, and attractive. This is not the issue. The issue is the definition of true love. If Scripture is true that God is love, then how can someone truly understand love apart from knowing Christ intimately (see 1 John 4:8)?

It may bring clarity to your situation to ask some penetrating questions about your love interest. What makes him tick? What consumes her? Is it a love for Christ and his church? Does he take delight in God's Word? Is she willing to stand up for truth even when it is not popular? Is he humble and quick to ask for forgiveness? Does she pray for you? Unbelievers don't just mess up and fail at these tasks. They are fundamentally unable to love the Lord and obey Christ in faith (see Rom. 8:7).

True love is soul deep. You want the kind of love that still stirs at old wrinkles. You want to clasp hands in the nursing home with a committed believer who has lived vigorously for the glory of God. An unbeliever doesn't have what it takes to keep cultivating long-term attraction to such wrinkles. Charm is deceitful, and beauty is fleeting, but a man or woman who fears the Lord is to be praised (see Prov. 31:30).

DATING ISN'T THE PLACE FOR DARKNESS

I wrote in a previous letter that God is the author of romance. It is true that to be in a romantic relationship is to be involved in something that God designed for good. God is the fiercest lover of all, and his love is the purest we can possibly imagine. Romance is one of the most intimate pursuits we can know as humans. Since it is so deeply personal and life altering, there should be no room for darkness in our dating life. What do light and darkness have in common? Nothing. Light is designed to put away darkness (see 2 Cor. 6:14).

We are called to be lights to the world; we are not called to let darkness into our lives. This is especially true for areas in which we covenant together. Although it can be hard to see when you are in the midst of a relationship, to date an unbeliever is to invite darkness into a room in which only light was meant to dwell.

It is one thing to share a meal with an unbelieving friend, but it is a completely different matter to contemplate exchanging vows of marriage with them. The believer and the unbeliever disagree on the most important reality in the universe: God.

ROMANCE ISN'T OFFENSIVE

Finally, flirting to convert ultimately fails because it is not offensive enough. The apostle Paul says that the cross is offensive (see 1 Cor. 1:18–25). The cross is gruesome because it calls the world to forsake all and to treasure God first and foremost. The cross requires repentance on our part, and this is offensive to our selfish desires. Holding hands is not hideous. Red roses are not repulsive. Whispering "sweet nothings" is not offensive.

Dating an unbeliever is actually one of the most unloving acts we can do for them. It is actually the opposite of evangelism. It says, "I value you more than I value what Christ says." It brings confusion where there should be a clear call to repentance.

Evangelistic dating is dangerous because it can exalt the gift over the Giver. Who wouldn't want to convert in order to marry the person they are crazy about? Who wouldn't want to say yes to Jesus in order for their significant other to say yes to them? God doesn't want to be a carrot on a stick. He wants people to come and die at his feet in order to find life (see Luke 14:26).

WHAT TO DO IF YOU ARE IN A RELATIONSHIP WITH AN UNBELIEVER

I believe you should start seeking advice from your local church on how to best end the relationship. The call of the hour is to speak the truth in love to the person you are dating (see Eph. 4:15). The call of repentance must be clear, and you must not be the prize if they turn away from sin. You will need to spend time explaining the gospel and pointing out the deep chasm of worldviews between the two of you. They need to know how different your thinking is on the most important issues in life and why this is a deal breaker.

Ending a relationship does not mean ending a friendship, but it does mean ending all romance. It will serve the person you are dating best if you point them to Christ instead of continuing to kindle feelings for them. Who knows? This obedience to God may be the means that Christ uses to revolutionize their life for the gospel. If so, praise God—but don't move back into the romantic relationship immediately. Growth requires time, and baby trees need more than one night to bear fruit.

I realize that these ideas may be challenging and difficult to process if you are deeply invested in a relationship with a non-Christian. As you contemplate them and then take the next step, I pray that the strength of Christ will enable and sustain you. The Lord guarantees to give you grace for even the most difficult commands. He is your strong Shepherd, and his goodness and mercy will follow you all the days of your life (see Ps. 23).

Until then,
Sean

DISCUSSION QUESTIONS

1. What are three qualities a believer possesses that an unbeliever does not?
2. Why is it unloving to date an unbeliever?
3. Who is a godly friend or mentor who can help you take the next necessary steps in your romantic relationship?

FIRST DATE

Spencer and Taylor

Dear Romantic,

Dating is often an escapade aimed at nothing. Some guy sees a girl, thinks she's cute and wants to have some fun, and asks her out. No intentions, no purpose, no end in sight.

You could respond to this in a variety of ways. On the one hand, you could shrug it off and say there's nothing inherently wrong with a simple date. Don't be so serious—lighten up. After all, you don't have to be certain that you're going to get married in order to take someone out. On the other hand, you could shun it off and say that Christians should abandon the entire concept of dating. Aimless "dating" is dangerous, hurtful, and selfish. Why even use the name *dating* when it carries so much baggage? Christians shouldn't be worldly, right? Are we really helping singles when we use the same term that the world uses?

Shrugging and shunning simply will not work. Adopting the purposeless and worldly notions of dating ignores the call of Scripture to put others above yourself and not to insist on your own way (see Phil. 2:3; 1 Cor. 13:4–5). Shunning dating tends to put more focus on the title of romance rather than on the heart of romance—what God really cares about.

God is concerned with our lives, our hearts, and our thoughts much more than he is concerned about the titles we use for our relationships. What matters most is not what you *call* a relationship, but who you are *in* it.

So how do you go about getting to know someone whom you find interesting? The answer is to explore with purpose.

DRIVEN BY PURPOSE

Purpose sets the parameters for you when you explore a relationship. What makes a first date honorable to God and the other person is when both of you have a genuine desire to know each other (see Rom. 12:9). We honor God when we ask questions aimed at understanding someone's character, because God cares more about our internal character than our external charm (see Prov. 31:30). This values what God values and thus glorifies God.

Purpose also keeps you on track. Few people want to be in an endless cycle of first dates without ever defining a relationship. When you have a purpose on those first dates, you gain clarity on whether or not to proceed into a more serious relationship. The Bible is full of descriptions of godly men and women (see 1 Tim. 3:1–7; 1 Peter 3:1–6). These descriptions show us what we should look for on those first dates. For example, as you get to know him, do you see a man who is growing in self-control (see 1 Tim. 3:2)? As you get to know her, do you see a women who cares more about her inward beauty than her looks (see 1 Pet. 3:4)? This makes your first date a time for you to grow in your understanding of the other person rather than a high-pressure environment in which you both try to impress each other.

Purpose sets you free from the unbiblical expectations that surround first dates. Instead of saying, "How do you make me feel when I am with you?" purpose says, "I know that God has been working in your life and growing you up until now, and I would love to learn more about it." Having a purpose helps you to assess a first date by the character of the person rather than their ability to create butterflies in your stomach.

ROOM TO EXPLORE

As important as purpose is, it sometimes chokes the life out of a first date. It's emotionally exhausting and unrealistic for you both to expect deep certainty about pursuing a relationship after just one dinner. First dates are for exploring the possibility of taking more steps and more dates. Although we plant a seed in the ground in the hope of receiving a flower, we don't dig up the seed from the ground because it does not produce a flower after one day. We water it, allow it to be nourished by the sun, and patiently await the harvest. In the same way, you should not allow your ultimate purpose in dating to choke the life out of your first date. In other words, you should not pick out your wedding colors after that first coffee together.

This means that it's okay to be unsure after your first date and to still agree to a second date. Uncertainty after your first date doesn't mean that you need to call it off. It means you are human. People are complex and take time to get to know. It's unloving to assume that you know everything about someone after just one date.

This does not mean that you should continue going on dates with someone even if you have absolutely no desire to move forward. This is where your purpose governs your exploration. Your purpose in your first dates is to decide whether or not to pursue a serious relationship aimed at marriage. If it is clear after one date that you do not want to be married to this person, then you should decline another date. Your exploration and purpose have merged and resulted in a clear decision.

Exploration must be governed by your purpose, and your purpose must be partnered with exploration.

This does not mean that everything will be clear after a few times spent with someone. It does, however, keep you from spending an eternity in dating limbo or from prematurely ending a good thing. Exploring with purpose lends itself to a smooth transition, an intentional relationship, or (if things don't work out) a normal friendship. In either case, see these first dates together as a privilege to be able to know the story of another child of God. Make it your goal to push this child toward ever-increasing conformity to Christ.

Until then,
Spencer and Taylor

DISCUSSION QUESTIONS

1. Are you more tempted to shrug or to shun the idea of dating? Why?
2. Which biblical character qualities do you think are most important to look for in a potential partner?

DECLINING A DATE

Sean and Jenny

Dear Sister,

Without a doubt, girls can be placed in an awkward position when they are asked out. Many times they are put on the spot, and the pressure to respond can escalate rather quickly. Perhaps you know this feeling and have later regretted your response. Is there a loving way for a girl to turn a guy down? Can a woman serve her brother in Christ when he goes out on a limb to ask her out?

The Bible is sufficient to help us reflect the glory of God in every area of our lives. The apostle Paul tells us that whether we eat or drink, or whatever we do, we should do it all to the glory of God (see 1 Cor. 10:31). This includes the moment when you are faced with saying no to a pursuer. Thankfully, there is a biblical way to turn a guy down. Christ can help us in even the most uncomfortable of moments.

COMPASSION: DECLINE AS YOU WOULD WANT TO BE DECLINED

One biblical truth you should apply to this situation is "Love your neighbor as yourself" (Matt. 22:39). Because we believe that God calls men to lead in the home, we are convinced it is the biblical role of the man to pursue the woman. Leadership requires initiative and risk—so if a guy doesn't have the courage to ask you out in person, he is not worth your time. But even if a guy finds himself asked out on a date by a girl, the principles in this chapter can still be applied. So let's reverse the roles for just a moment and ask, "How would I want to be declined?"

If you were nervous and your voice was trembling as you asked out the person of your dreams, how would you want to be turned down? Graciously? Abruptly? Flippantly? If you are in the position of being asked out, it is likely because the guy found you attractive and enjoyable to be around. This is an honor! With the grace of Christ, you can decline a romantic offer in a way that is kind and shows that you are truly flattered he would ask you on a date.

Declining a date doesn't have to involve *only* pain. It can also be an opportunity to build someone else up. There is a way to build up your brother when you decline his date (see 1 Thess. 5:11). Even if you are totally caught off guard when he asks you out, you can let him know that you appreciate the offer and are thankful for him.

CLEAR INTENTIONS AND A CONCISE RESPONSE

Many girls feel bad saying no to a guy. In order to lessen the blow, they will often leave the door open for the future.

Many compassionate girls unintentionally offer guys hope that romance might be kindled in the future, even though they have zero interest in a future relationship. Although it is hard, it is *loving* to seal the door shut if you are not romantically interested in somebody.

Being clear and concise is like ripping a Band-Aid off quickly—it may hurt, but the pain lasts for only a few seconds and is worth it. You don't want to create a saga that drags on for weeks when you could have handled the situation in a few seconds.

When you decline a romantic relationship, it is important to speak the *truth* in love (see Eph. 4:25–29). If you are truly not interested, then do not hint at future possibilities. Though you might be fearful, be clear with your intentions and state that you are only interested in friendship. If you are tempted to keep talking (in order to break the awkwardness of the moment), graciously change the subject. It is important not to hide behind an excuse that really isn't truthful. There is no need to fear man when you fear God.

Here is a summary of some common responses:

- "It's not God's will for me right now." While this statement may have good intentions, it actually places the blame on God and dodges ownership. God directs his people through the Bible and through the desires he gives us as we walk daily in fellowship with him. If you know it is not God's will because you don't desire it, it is more helpful to be up front and communicate that friendship is the only option on the table.
- "It's not the right time." Say this only if you want to be asked out again next month by the same guy. It would be more helpful to say that you are grateful, but not interested

in a romantic relationship. Leave the door cracked only if you want it to be opened again.

- "I'm not ready to date anyone yet." If this is true, then it is good to be humble and admit this. However, this can also leave a kernel of hope for a guy to dwell on for the next several months. If you are not ready to date yet and you know that you would never date the guy who asked you out, you should be up front and not use this as an alibi. It is better to tell him that you are not interested in a relationship with him.

WHAT IF THEY ASK WHY YOU DECLINED?

Another scenario is possible: A guy asks you out and catches you a little off guard. You agree with everything we just said above and try to say something that is compassionate, clear, and concise. You respond, "I am thankful for your offer. That is very kind that you would ask me. I am going to say no, but I am thankful for you as my brother in Christ." There is an awkward silence, and then the guy asks for a reason. He wants to know why you are turning him down. What should you do?

As the wisest man on earth once said, there is a time for everything (see Eccl. 3:1). There is a time to speak, and there is a time not to speak. It all depends on what would be most loving to tell him and what would serve him the best in the long term.

Depending on the situation and the nature of the friendship, we can imagine a scenario in which it *is loving* to explain *why* you are not interested. Perhaps he is immature in a particular area spiritually and could really benefit from hearing a compassionate reason why you are not interested in him romantically. You will need to exercise wisdom before responding like this.

Does the guy have a soft heart and ears to hear from you? Would he benefit from knowing about a particular area in his life that requires growth? This may demand an extra measure of boldness on your part, but feel free to treat him as your brother in Christ.

If he is asking for clarification, you can share your concerns with him honestly and lovingly. You can let him know that you are honored but have noticed particular areas in his life that give you pause. Let's say the issue is that he is undisciplined and doesn't manage his time well. You could mention that you have noticed specific ways in which he is neglecting responsibilities at work and in his spiritual life. You can reassure him that you are not a superior but are a sister in Christ. You can also let him know that you are not sharing this reason with other people but are only telling him this because he asked for clarification.

There are other times when it would simply be more loving to remain clear and concise without offering a specific reason. For instance, if you don't find him physically attractive, then you don't need to share that information with him. It would be obviously unloving to say, "I don't think you are attractive." Instead, you can stand your ground by saying something like, "Thank you again for asking, but I am simply not interested in a romantic relationship together. I am thankful to be your friend, but that is all that is available." If you shower him with kindness and repeat yourself again, it is likely he will get the point and conclude that it is best for him not to know the reason.

No one wants to be turned down, but everyone wants to be treated with compassion and honesty. If you are going to turn a guy down, God will give you grace to do so in a way that glorifies Christ. Ask the Lord for help as you seek to honor your brother during those uncomfortable moments. He will appreciate your kindness and will value you all the more as his sister in Christ. I am thankful that you desire to glorify God whether you eat, drink, or decline a date.

Until then,
Sean and Jenny

DISCUSSION QUESTIONS

1. When declining a date, are you tempted to be *unclear* or *unkind*? Why do you lean toward that approach?
2. Write out, in a clear and kind way, your own sample paragraph for politely declining a date.

SHOULD WE BE IN
A RELATIONSHIP?

Sean

Dear Romantic,

How should a Christian think about another Christian when it comes to a potential romance? Perhaps a guy is about to pursue someone or a girl is considering a possible relationship. The answer to this question must be thought through biblically and practically. Although these categories are not exhaustive, they may be helpful for you as you think about a potential spouse. I have found that there are four main ingredients for Christian "chemistry."

1. CHARACTER

It need not go without saying: when it comes to marriage, godly character is not just a deal breaker; it is what the game is all about. It is our joy, as Christians, to be conformed into the image of Jesus (see Rom. 8:29). Character outlasts charm, and godliness goes beyond goosebumps. Whoever you marry will either help you love Jesus more or pour water on your fire for God. If Paul was right in 1 Corinthians 15:33 about bad company corrupting good character, then I guarantee that your spouse will impact your spiritual life. You don't just spend an hour or two a week with your spouse; you eat, drink, and sleep with them.

Character is first on the list because, without it, nothing else matters. This is the sun that all planets orbit around. Without a deep love for Jesus, marriage will be miserable. The potential wife should be maturing into a Proverbs 31 woman and the potential husband into a Psalm 112 man.

It also should be noted that there is a difference between potential godliness and actual godliness. A wise friend once told me that potential godliness does not exist. It is simply "potential." The person you are considering for marriage must have real, visible godly character.

A woman needs a husband who is maturing in the faith in order to lead her closer to Jesus. Perfection is not required, but pursuit of holiness is mandatory. A man should be seeking a woman who is already exhibiting love, compassion, wisdom, and gentleness. He should look for a girl who is already serving in her church. She will be a keeper.

Consider asking some questions: Will this man teach my children the Scriptures? Will this woman raise my children to love the Lord? Is this man a role model whom I want to follow? Is this lady someone who can show me more of God's heart and push me closer to Christ? Will you be able to count on this person when chaos and calamity hit your life?

2. HARMONY

Not everyone is meant to get along all the time. It is a sin to have ungodly character (see 1 Tim. 3), but it is not a sin to be socially incompatible. Perhaps you are an extrovert and can't help but be the life of the party. You may or may not mesh with the introvert who loves studying instead of singing karaoke. If you love hiking, rock climbing, and adventuring in the outdoors, you might not want to marry someone who is content never to see sunlight. Then again, that kind of thing just might stoke your fire. To each his own.

The point is that you need to marry someone you can have a happy conversation with, someone who enjoys at least some of the things that you do. Marriage is not meant to be miserable. The best way to figure out whether your personalities mesh well together is to spend time together in as many appropriate settings as possible.

This harmony is important in areas such as theology, politics, and commitment to children. If you are a Presbyterian and your fiancé is a Baptist, there may be murky waters ahead. You will need to have many conversations about your beliefs on church government, spiritual gifts, and the inerrancy of Scripture. The more you talk about now, the better. You may discover that you both were predestined to get married or that you should freely choose to abandon the relationship.[1]

3. TRAJECTORY

It is not enough just to be godly and personable. The man needs to have a plan. What will you be doing in the near future?

1. A helpful guide can be found online at John Piper, "Questions to Ask When Preparing for Marriage," Desiring God, August 6, 2009, http://www.desiringgod.org/articles/questions-to-ask-when-preparing-for-marriage. This is a list of over fifty important questions couples should ask each other. Jenny and I enjoyed working through these questions and tried to discuss two or three questions every date.

You need to be seeking the Lord and to be conscious of the direction you are traveling. How are you going to bring glory to Jesus with the days he has given you?

A woman should not marry a man who is simply blowing in the wind. As a woman, do you want to follow the man you are interested in? Do you want to submit to his leadership and pursue magnifying Jesus together? If he wants to be a construction worker who shares the gospel while on a forklift, are you okay with raising his hard-hat family? If he wants to be a missionary to Alaska, have you warmed up to the idea of wearing a parka?

Do your visions of life align? Are you okay with moving away from your parents? What areas of ministry are you passionate about? What do you picture your future family looking like? Do you want to work in or out of the home? How do you envision spending your money? Are you of one mind, as Philippians 2:2 says? Don't talk about just the big things. Talk about the small and medium-sized issues as well.

4. ATTRACTION

Your future spouse should be your best friend on the planet. But a spouse needs to be more than this. If you come home from work and only want to play checkers together, we have a problem. The Bible commands spouses to delight sexually in each other, and this requires a level of physical attraction (see Prov. 5:18–19).

Notice that attraction is last on this list. I place it last because attraction can be automatic or it can be cultivated. You may be interested in someone simply because they caught your eye. This is not necessarily a problem. However, don't underestimate the fact that physical attraction can also be cultivated.

It's funny how this works. Attraction can blind people to ungodly character. "Do not desire her beauty in your heart, and do not let her capture you with her eyelashes" (Prov. 6:25). Yet godly character can open eyes to see beauty. "But let your adorning be the hidden person of the heart with the imperishable beauty of a gentle and quiet spirit, which in God's sight is very precious" (1 Pet. 3:4). That beauty can spill over into physical interest.

You may not be swooning over someone the first time you see them, but after you notice this person's character, personality, and trajectory in life . . . you might be surprised to find yourself growing in physical affection for them. Sexual attraction can begin with an initial flash, or it can slowly build into a boil.

For those who are currently dealing with pornography, lust, or same-sex attraction, it is important to mention that dating is not the solution to sexual sin. Dating is not designed by God to be the vehicle by which a person's sexual desires are transformed. Being in a relationship with someone in order to change sexual attraction or to ultimately satisfy sexual cravings misses the message of the Bible. Sexual purity in both thought and deed is the biblical standard for everyone. Christ—not a marriage covenant—enables us to obtain sexual purity.[2]

All of this underscores the importance of walking openly in a Christian community. It is never good to experiment in a lab late at night without telling anyone. Professors assign lab partners for a reason. You need the body of Christ to help you evaluate character, compatibility, trajectory, and attraction in the context of

2. Two helpful resources on the topic of sexual sin and purity are Joshua Harris, *Sex Is Not the Problem (Lust Is): Sexual Purity in a Lust-Saturated World* (Colorado Springs: Multnomah, 2005), and Denny Burk and Heath Lambert, *Transforming Homosexuality: What the Bible Says about Sexual Orientation and Change* (Phillipsburg, NJ: P&R, 2015).

your relationship. Invite the church into your life, and don't be afraid to ask your church whether or not you are concocting the right ingredients in your Christian chemistry.

Until then,
Sean

DISCUSSION QUESTIONS

1. Which ingredients (character, harmony, trajectory, attraction) do you and your partner currently have together? Which areas are you unsure about?
2. Are there any incomplete ingredients in your relationship? How could these areas be improved or strengthened?
3. List two older people who could begin mentoring you and your partner.

ON PARENTS

Spencer

Dear Romantic,

Life enters into an awkward transitional phase when your relationship gets serious. You move into a strange halfway house in which your single self and your "potentially married" self must occupy the same space. It's not yet *his* responsibility to lead, but he finds himself in more situations where *she* wants him to decide. It's not yet *her* responsibility to submit, but she finds herself trusting him more as *he* leads. Neither are biblically commanded to do this, but it becomes comfortable and compelling as time goes on. As the season of your relationship begins to change and your confidence grows, your single self and married self seem to be less comfortable in the same room—and things can get tense.

For many adult couples, this tension is strongest when it comes to their relationship with their parents. The tension comes from the fact that individuals in a dating relationship are called to honor their parents (see Eph. 6:1; Col 3:20) but are also exploring a reality that would take them out from under their authority (see Gen. 2:24; Eph. 5:31). For most couples and parents, this is tender and uncharted territory.

The tension grows when the parents are hesitant, suspicious, or completely disapproving of the relationship. Most loving parents, whether or not they are believers, long to have some role in their child's romantic relationship. And if these parents are believers, they have a God-given command to shepherd their children until they are married (Eph. 6:4). When children have parents who they generally respect, they long for their parents' blessing. Add to this the scriptural command to honor and obey your parents (see Eph. 6:1–2).

How should you respond when your parents are hesitant about or disapproving of your relationship?

INCLINE YOUR EAR

When a Christian parent raises a red flag or gives a word of caution about a relationship, our sinful reflex can be to respond with disdain. How could they seek to uproot this blossoming romance? But the biblical reflex to parental caution is not disdain, but inclination. The entire book of Proverbs is a series of red flags, cautions, and directions given from a parent to a child. And the refrain of these instructions is to "hear . . . your father's instruction, and forsake not your mother's teaching" (Prov. 1:8).

As your parents share their concerns about your relationship, are you listening? Instead of having an immediate response of defense and disdain, listen well and listen long. Even if your parents don't understand your relationship completely, and even if they aren't believers, it's important for you to incline your ear when they raise a concern.

That being said, inclining your ear does not mean agreeing

that your parents are faultless or have a perfectly accurate view of your relationship. Many couples have parents who are non-Christians and may oppose a relationship *because* their son or daughter is considering marrying another Christian. These couples should *not* listen to any advice that directly opposes Scripture. Our loyalty must be to Jesus over our families (see Matt. 10:37), and his Word must govern the direction of our relationship.

But how do you incline your ear to your parents when they love you, love God's Word, and also disapprove of your relationship?

HONORING AND EVALUATING

Before you enter into a potentially difficult season in your relationship with your parents, it's important for you to get clear on what God expects of you. God expects you to *honor* your parents. This means assuming the best about your parents' motives, considering their concerns, and speaking well about them to others.

When it feels like your relationship is being attacked, it's tempting to assume that whoever is doing the attacking must be your enemy. But this assumes that your parents' motive is to destroy rather than to build. Love believes, hopes, and bears all things (see 1 Cor. 13:7). If you assume that your parents' disapproval is motivated by malice, it will breed suspicion in your soul. But if you believe the best about your parents' motives, it will breed a gentle demeanor that pushes away anger (see Prov. 15:1).

Taking this humble posture toward your parents allows you to consider their concerns biblically. Unless your parents have identified obvious sin in your relationship, their concerns will most likely fall into the category of wisdom. This means that your parents may not share specific ways they believe your relationship violates Scripture, but they may identify some gaps in your perspective that you can't see. One excellent way to evaluate whether or not wisdom is biblical is to think through the picture of wisdom in James 3:17: "But the wisdom from above is first pure, then peaceable, gentle, open to reason, full of mercy and good fruits, impartial and sincere." Ask yourself these questions:

- Is there any objective reason to believe that my parents' concerns are defiled or impure due to ill motive or misinformation? Can I provide them with additional information that they are missing?
- Are my parents' concerns being presented in a peaceful way rather than in a combative way?
- Are my parents gentle, or harsh, toward our relationship?
- Are my parents open to new information about my relationship that may change their perspective, or are they closed to any new insight?
- Would the fruit of heeding my parents' wisdom result in any unbiblical outcome?
- As best as I can tell, are these concerns aimed at our well-being and good?

Obviously, no parent will perfectly meet all the biblical qualifications of wisdom. For example, it's possible your parents may be speaking accurately about your relationship, and with biblical wisdom, but may also be communicating with a sinful tone or attitude. It is possible to speak the truth without love. But are your parents' concerns generally characterized by these categories? If so, it is best for you to heed their cautions and concerns.

LOVING WHILE LEAVING

However, there are couples who, after honoring and evaluating, believe that their parents' concerns and cautions are not wise. How can couples who want to honor their parents do so without heeding their parents' concerns?

The answer is for couples to move forward *only under* God-given authority. Outside Jesus himself, this authority is the local church. Christians are to be subject to the leaders of their church (see 1 Peter 5:5). And these leaders are given the responsibility to shepherd their souls (see 1 Peter 5:2).

Before you take the next step in your relationship, share your parents' concerns with a pastor in your church. Seek to share their concerns accurately and fairly, and ask for the pastor's honest counsel for you and your significant other. A pastor or church leader should also meet with your parents in order to hear their perspective. If you find that this pastor or leader agrees with your parents, you should reconsider your parents' concerns. But if he believes that you have handled the situation biblically and that your relationship is godly and good for you, then you gain confidence under the authority of your local church.

KEEP PRESSING

When parents and young couples disagree about the direction of a relationship, it can leave scars. Parents get hurt; couples feel misunderstood. Before you begin walking down this path, resolve to be committed to your relationship with your parents. If they are taking the time to share their concerns, they are most likely doing so out of a loving heart and sincere concern for you. Although these conversations may be difficult for you and them, let this journey *refine* rather than *define* your relationship in the future. And, in time, our good God will use this for your and your parents' good.

Until then,
Spencer

DISCUSSION QUESTIONS

1. What are your parents saying about your relationship? Have they shared any concerns with you? If so, what are they?
2. Review the wisdom evaluation questions above. Are your parents' concerns wise? Why or why not?
3. When and how you will share your answers to questions 1 and 2 with a leader or mentor in your church?

DATING AND PORNOGRAPHY

Sean

Dear Romantic,

Many people who are pursuing a relationship also struggle with pornography. For those who have looked at pornographic images during a romantic relationship, this is a critical issue that cannot be ignored. For those who struggle with pornography, certain fears can abound: What if someone finds out? What will my partner think? Can I really change? How will this affect my future marriage? What if I can never be free?

If you are serious about your romantic relationship and your relationship with the Lord, then serious action must be taken. Later in life, you do not want to turn over in bed next to your spouse and search for porn on your iPhone. Nor do you want to shrug off this sin and then turn over in the flames of hell. When it comes to sexual sin, hands must be cut off and eyes must be gouged out (see Matt. 5:29–30). Pornography is not a pet to stroke, but a snake to crush. How you respond to this sin leads to either life or death. Yet there is a greater gospel reality that we must realize.

Many Christians do not realize the power they have been granted to fight even their darkest desires. When Christ screamed in agony on the wooden tree, he did not scream in vain. The strength that surged through the veins of Jesus now surges through you by the gift of the Holy Spirit. Christ has come to set you free, and you can be free indeed (see John 8:36). There is no porn pit too deep for the light of Christ to reach. Christ is risen from the dead, and he gives immeasurable power to those who believe (see Eph. 1:19). Come into the light and believe that there is power in the precious blood of the Lamb.

At this point you might be wondering, *Should we continue dating? Should I postpone proposing because of porn?* These are complex questions, but they *must* be answered. The first order of business is to bring in a wise counselor. I am not involved enough in your daily life to give hand-tailored advice. You will need someone who can speak directly into your life, assess the scenario, examine your fruit, and help you make the call. You need a referee on the field rather than a commentator from the stands.

But, from my aerial viewpoint, here is what I have noticed. There are two kinds of people who struggle with pornography: those who are slaves to Jesus and those who are slaves to Satan; those who have the Holy Spirit in them and those who do not. You must examine yourself and take inventory of your soul.

Are you enslaved to pornography and making little or no progress in your spiritual life? Or are you struggling but growing in grace and gaining victory? If you are consumed with porn and know it, ending your relationship (or at least postponing engagement until you are able to get adequate help) must be on the table. For the man who is enslaved to porn, marriage is not the answer—Jesus is.

If you are tempted to look at pornography but not enslaved

to it, delaying engagement might not be the best counsel. When talking with a counselor, you should discuss how long you have experienced victory and how broken you are over your sin. Marriage is not the solution to porn, but it certainly can help. If you burn with passion, it is good to marry (see 1 Cor. 7:9). But in order for you to qualify for marriage, you must be fighting this sin vigorously and seeing Jesus give you noticeable victory in battle. The marriage bed is to be undefiled (see Heb. 13:4).

Discovering a tumor and removing it is painful and frightening. Yet everyone would trade the short-term pain of surgery for a cancer-free body. Sin thrives in secret. Mold, bacteria, and fungi all fester in dark places—and porn is just like them. Confession may be a brief pain, but it brings sweet relief. Every broken porn addict who comes to Christ in faith will never be turned away. God creates a clean heart and renews a right spirit (see Ps. 51:10). Confess your sin to God and then to a strong Christian leader in your life. God has given us pastors and mentors to help us grow in godliness. They will welcome you with open arms and strengthen you in the faith.

The difficult part comes when it is time to talk with your boyfriend or girlfriend. You cannot wait until the day after you take engagement photos. You don't want to pop the question and then spring this on him or her. That would not be fair. It is better to bring this issue up sooner rather than later.

Great care and wisdom must be exercised when you tell your partner. Pray for the next available opportunity. Inform your partner that you are relying upon Jesus and fighting this temptation with all his might. Talk about how you hate sin and how Jesus is helping you overcome it. Make sure that you are clear but not overly detailed. Do not tell all the grit and grime of your struggle. Even if your partner wants to know, it will not build them up to talk about what you watched and how long you stared at others naked. State the struggle, tell who is holding you accountable, explain your plan to "bear fruit in keeping with repentance" (Matt. 3:8), and ask for prayer and grace.

I want to encourage you to confess this sin to those whom you trust regardless of any consequences that you might be fearful of reaping. "Do not fear those who kill the body but cannot kill the soul. Rather fear him who can destroy both soul and body in hell" (Matt. 10:28). There has never been a better time to draw near to the God who loves you. Rest assured that as you walk toward him in the light, he won't turn you away. As you draw near to God, he will draw near to you. Listen to these words from James 4:7–10.

> Submit yourselves therefore to God. Resist the devil, and he will flee from you. Draw near to God, and he will draw near to you. Cleanse your hands, you sinners, and purify your hearts, you double-minded. Be wretched and mourn and weep. Let your laughter be turned to mourning and your joy to gloom. Humble yourselves before the Lord, and he will exalt you.

Shrivel your sin in the light, cut off all temptation, and run to the risen Savior.

I have watched as pornography has ravished the minds of dear friends, leaving them lonely and cold. I don't want that for you. I am confident in the Lord that you can put this to death. Christ has overcome the grave, and pornography is no match for our resurrected Lord. Take hope in his power, which can cut any chain (see John 8:34–36).

Until then,
Sean

DISCUSSION QUESTIONS

1. Who in your life knows about this struggle? How are they holding you accountable? If you have looked at pornography recently, who is a stronger, more mature Christian you can talk to about this?
2. Are there any immediate steps you can take to cut off the temptation to view pornography?
3. Does your boyfriend or girlfriend know about this area of your life?
4. For further reading on this topic, read Heath Lambert's excellent book *Finally Free: Fighting for Purity with the Power of Grace* (Grand Rapids: Zondervan, 2013).

DO WE HAVE A BAD RELATIONSHIP?

Sean

Dear Romantic,

Have you ever ridden in a car with someone who believes that a yellow light is always a sign to speed up? Perhaps you are this person. You are two hundred feet away from the stoplight, and you see it change from green to yellow. The adrenaline pumps, and you push the pedal.

Yellow lights are a blessing from God. They are designed to minimize accidents by helping us decide whether to stop or keep going. Yellow lights are our friends even though they can be an inconvenience and annoyance.

In a similar way, there are signs that surface during relationships that should not be ignored. It is foolish to blaze through a yellow light without looking around and assessing the situation beforehand. In dating, there are some helpful warning signs that should be on our radar. These warnings should give us pause and should cause us to consider whether or not it is best to continue a relationship. Later we will talk about sexual sin, but right now

I want to address the warning signs of obsession, manipulation, and abuse.

WARNING SIGN #1: OBSESSION

When two people are attracted to each other and begin spending time together, it is possible to become infatuated with each other in a way that is unbiblical. It is not good when individuals begin to pour all their time, energy, thoughts, and money into a dating relationship to the detriment of faithfulness in other areas. Those involved in a dating relationship are not only boyfriend and girlfriend but also sons, daughters, church members, friends, evangelists, employees, and so on. Dating should not consume us to the point that we exclude obedience to God. In fact, I submit that this is unhealthy even in a marriage relationship.

The apostle Paul writes,

> This is what I mean, brothers: the appointed time has grown very short. From now on, *let those who have wives live as though they had none*, and those who mourn as though they were not mourning, and those who rejoice as though they were not rejoicing, and those who buy as though they had no goods, and those who deal with the world as though they had no dealings with it. For the present form of this world is passing away. (1 Cor. 7:29–31)

We know from other passages that Paul wrote (such as Eph. 5:22–33; 1 Cor. 7:5) that the Bible doesn't want spouses to neglect each other. But here in 1 Corinthians 7:29–31, Paul is saying that marriage isn't ultimately about your spouse. Instead, the focus of marriage should be looking forward to the marriage supper of the Lamb that will take place when Jesus returns (see

Rev. 19:6–10). The apostle Paul is reflecting exactly what Jesus taught in Luke 14:26: "If anyone comes to me and does not hate his own father and mother and *wife* and children and brothers and sisters, yes, and even his own life, he cannot be my disciple." Jesus wants our love for God to be so rich and vibrant that all our earthly loves look like hate in comparison. Simply put, Christian couples must be obsessed with Jesus above anyone else. A believer's greatest joy is delighting in the Creator, not worshiping the Creator's creation.

How do you know whether you are in an obsessive relationship? Ask yourself some of the following questions:

- Do you spend too much time with your partner to the exclusion of other Christian friendships? Is your partner okay with you spending time with other Christian friends? Do both of you have older men or women speaking into your lives?
- Are you or your partner easily offended when one of you doesn't tell the other small details about your plans? Do you or your partner have to know everything that is going on in each other's daily lives?
- Does your thought life focus only on your partner without reference to God?
- Are you suspicious of one another?
- Are you neglecting your local church?

WARNING SIGNS #2 AND #3: MANIPULATION OR ABUSE

No one sets out on a first date planning to enter into a relationship that eventually becomes filled with fear, regret, and misplaced power. A relationship that continues to be obsessive can eventually become manipulative or abusive. Terrifying statements can become cloaked in the form of "love." The following statements can send chills up the spine:

- "If you leave me, I will kill myself."
- "You won't ever be able to find a relationship like this one."
- "You are the only one who has ever loved me."

Perhaps you have never heard these statements, but you know the subtle ways they are communicated. You may feel the pressure to remain in the dating relationship, to go a little further physically, or maybe even to become numb to the physical force used against you. A relationship that is maintained by manipulation has lost all sight of true love.

Consider 1 Corinthians 13 and how it differs from a manipulative and abusive relationship: Love is patient, not pressuring. Love is kind, not harsh. Love doesn't control via envy. It is not rude, nor is it domineering. It is not self-seeking or demanding. It is not easily angered. Love keeps no record of wrongs and certainly doesn't hold them over a person's head. Love does not delight in doing harm, but rejoices with the truth. It always trusts and always protects. Love doesn't fail, even if a relationship comes to an end.

WHAT SHOULD YOU DO?

I don't know your exact situation, but if you find yourself in a relationship that is obsessive, manipulative, or abusive, there are at least four steps to finding relief.

First, get help. The first thing you should do is to reach out to someone who is trustworthy and more mature than you. You need people to speak truth and clear away the fog. It is incredibly difficult to discern the right thing to do when you have been slowly immersed in a relationship with someone you love. You need a godly third party who can provide an honest and helpful assessment of your situation.

Second, if you have been abused, get out. Don't buy the lie that you deserve abuse. Don't believe for a second that you are responsible for your partner's actions. Reach out immediately to a spiritual authority to get relief. The most loving thing you can do for your partner is to help them get help. No matter how much you are threatened, you can be free and can find relief. Now is the time to get out of your dating relationship. If your partner has threatened to commit suicide, it is imperative that you find someone who can help them. You are not their savior, and you are not meant to carry the burdens that they force on you. Pray and ask God for strength to reach out to a pastor, parent, certified biblical counselor, or all of the above.

Third, ask Jesus for forgiveness for any known sin. If you have focused too much on the other person and have treated them like an idol, ask God to forgive you and to help you change. If you now realize that you have been pressured into things you regret or have been caught up in a relationship to the exclusion of God, now is the time to repent. You can ask God for grace to change and to help refocus your attention in life.

Fourth, if you realize you have sinned against your partner, ask for forgiveness. If you have been in a manipulative relationship, you need much wisdom from trusted advisors in order to know the best way to do this. However, if you have been domineering and controlling, you must make things right before God and others. Don't be so proud that you are unable to admit you have made mistakes. We all have sinned and fallen short of the glory of God (see Rom. 3:23). You can confess your sin and by grace begin leading in a way that is reflective of divine, selfless love.

Yellow lights should not be ignored. It isn't safe or wise to plow through an intersection without taking proper assessment of the situation. If you see the yellow lights of obsession or manipulation in yourself or in your partner, I exhort you to slam on the breaks. Do not risk plowing through a red light in your relationship. By coming to a complete stop, you will likely avoid a collision, and you may even realize that you need to get out of the car.

Until then,
Sean

DISCUSSION QUESTIONS

1. Does your relationship involve any obsession, manipulation, or abuse? If so, how often do these things take place, and how severe are they?
2. What mature person can help you find clarity in your dating relationship?
3. What are your fears about ending your current dating relationship?
4. If you don't know anyone who can help you, search for a certified counselor from the Association of Certified Biblical Counselors online at www.biblicalcounseling.com.

BREAKING UP

Spencer

Dear Romantic,

You have sought counsel, struggled to discern your desires, and had numerous conversations with your partner. There have been tears, anxiety, and stress—but now you have clarity. You have made the decision to end your relationship.

Breaking up is not an inherent sign of relational failure. You didn't "fail" at your relationship; you are not "losing" at the dating game; you are not "betraying" your partner. You don't need to go into panic mode and spend the next three days worrying about whether or not you have sinned. As we mentioned in previous chapters, some people do break up for sinful reasons or because of sin. But if you have sought to respect your partner, honor the Lord, and communicate clearly, there is nothing sinful about breaking up. It's actually the right thing to do.

All that being said, this is probably going to hurt. You and your partner may have spent several months together. You have built memories, shared mutual friends, and even attended church together. The initial effects of a breakup initiate a grieving process that provokes different responses. You don't know how your partner will respond, and you should not try to control their emotions. Your responsibility is to love your partner and to do to them as you would want them to do to you (see Matt. 7:12).

Before anything else, your partner is your neighbor and sibling in Christ. As strange as it may sound, you are to break up with them as you would desire them to break up with you. You are to speak the truth to your partner because you are "members of one another" (Eph. 4:25). Difficulty and righteousness often walk hand in hand, and just as you have gained clarity in your desire to step away from this relationship, the right thing to do is tell the truth to your partner with clarity and charity.

CLARITY AND CHARITY

Ambiguity in a breakup adds salt to a wound. Speak clearly with your partner about *why* you have decided to end your relationship. Wisdom from above is *reasonable* (see James 3:17). Before you enter into this conversation, take time to think through why you are ending the relationship. Give one or two significant reasons to your partner concerning this decision, and speak to them with kindness and truth. Realize that this will be painful for your partner to hear. Don't seek to make less of it or try to cheer your partner up if he or she responds in sadness. He who sings to a heavy heart is like someone who takes off another's garment on a cold day (see Prov. 25:20). Speak the truth, and speak it clearly.

Although clarity is important, it kills when it isn't seasoned with charity and consideration. You can tell the truth perfectly but still cause unnecessary pain to your partner because you *overload* them with the truth. Wisdom seeks to speak a *fitting word* and to give an *apt answer* when communicating difficult truths (see Prov. 15:23; 25:11). Don't feel the need to give all the reasons that you are ending the relationship. There may be many factors to your decision, but unless your partner is demanding more, provide only one or two reasons.

As a side note, it will serve your partner if you consider where and when you are going to have this conversation. Don't plan to bring it up at the end of an otherwise fun date night. You don't want to blindside your partner. Communicate up front that you want to have a serious conversation with him or her. It's also helpful to be in a private place with an easy exit. Everyone responds differently to hurt, and giving your partner a private space to talk and ask questions without interruption, as well as an easy exit to leave, will serve best in the end.

FACING THE TENSION

As you give this news to your partner, you will feel a tension. Although you are ending your relationship, you may feel the tug to care for them in the same way that you did when you were in the relationship. Although the relationship is ending, this does not mean you will be desensitized to the pain that your partner is experiencing. You may feel compelled to make promises, to qualify what you're saying, and to tell them that you will still be in their life. But if you are breaking up after a longer relationship, you should not promise the same closeness that you once had together.

Although you will feel this tension, resist it. Instead of trying to help your partner through this breakup, entrust your partner to the Lord and to the local church. After the breakup, it may be best to maintain a healthy distance from your partner. This allows for time to heal after what can be an emotionally pain-ful time. This does not mean you should ignore them or treat them with cold distance when you see them after your breakup. Your interactions should be kind and warm. However, you must entrust them to God. He cares for them more than you ever will. Trust in the God who draws near to the brokenhearted and the crushed in spirit (see Ps. 34:18).

ENTRUSTING AND TRUSTING

Every Christian is a sheep that belongs to Jesus. He is the Good Shepherd who walks with his sheep through the deepest valleys (see Ps. 23). The same Shepherd who is walking with you through this difficult decision will remain close to your partner through their season of pain. And as time takes them through the valley, the presence of the Shepherd will be their peace. Although relationships end, Jesus promises that he will never leave or forsake you—through both this trial and those to come (see Heb. 13:5).

Until then,
Spencer

DISCUSSION QUESTIONS

1. What is more difficult for you: clarity or charity?
2. Is it more tempting to comfort your partner in an unhelpful way or to be cold toward them? Why?

BLAME AFTER A BREAKUP

Sean and Jenny

Dear Romantic,

There is nothing fun about a broken relationship. "Hope deferred makes the heart sick" (Prov. 13:12). After a breakup, you can experience a mixture of emotions and thoughts as sadness, guilt, and pain swirl together.

"I am not attractive." "I am not godly enough." "I deserve only bad relationships." "How could they do this to me?" "This is their fault." "They ruined everything."

Perhaps you have had these thoughts. The serpent can bite after a breakup. Satan is the serpent of slander, and he often whispers lies and deceit (see John 8:44; Rev. 12:10). Self-deprecation is a real temptation for many who have experienced heartbreak. Perhaps this describes your current experience. You might blame yourself or spend hours cross-examining every conversation from the relationship. The call of the hour is for the Spirit to align your thinking into conformity with the Scriptures.

The Scriptures tell us to take an honest assessment of our lives and not to think more highly of ourselves than we ought (see Rom.

12:3). There will always be areas in our walk with God in which we could be growing. Perhaps someone says that they broke up with you because of a character flaw or an area in your life that needs growth. The Bible wants us to learn from hard conversations and to grow in godliness. We should examine all criticism in light of the Scriptures and align ourselves with the revealed Word of God. For example, if your partner says that you tend to become very impatient, you should search the Bible for what it says about patience. Be humble and honest and assess where your heart is in this matter. Try not to put up a defense, but allow the Holy Spirit to work in your life and conform you to God's Son.

If an area of your character needs attention, the proper response is to repent and ask forgiveness from Christ and everyone you have sinned against in the process. Ask God for grace and to "work out your own salvation with fear and trembling" (see Phil. 2:12–13). It is true that we reap what we sow, but for the Christian this falls under the category of discipline, not punishment. We must be grounded in the reality that God does not punish his children. There is no condemnation for those who are in Christ (see Rom. 8:1). God never punishes his elect in either this life or the life to come. God is only *for* his people (see Rom. 8:28). The condemning lies of Satan must be combated with the believer's spotless forgiveness in Christ.

Breakups are a time for honest examination and then a total affirmation of the righteousness found in Christ. If there is room for spiritual growth after a relationship has ended, don't despair! God will give you more grace. Use this season as a healthy time to examine yourself in order to better your next relationship.

Those who have been "dumped" need to realize that they are not trash in God's eyes. This might not be your struggle, however. You might be harboring bitter thoughts or blame toward the person who broke up with you. In order to put away bitterness, you will need to show a 1 Corinthians 13 kind of love. Love keeps no record of wrongs and does not cast the first stone. You will need to make every effort to pursue peace as much as it depends on you and to be ready to extend forgiveness for any fault (see Rom. 12:18; Mark 11:25).

However, if sin was not involved during or after the relationship, don't overanalyze or become too introspective. We must beware of assuming that every breakup is due to sin. Job's suffering was not a result of sin, and not every breakup should be equated with bad living.

PHYSICAL APPEARANCE AND GODLINESS

"I must not be attractive" is perhaps the sneakiest of all the slanderous accusations of Satan. This lie snares many. The most damaging part of this lie is how people respond to it. If someone feels unattractive, he or she may seek fleshly solutions. Once this fruit is bitten, depression and then sexual immorality of some kind often follow. Believing this lie may also result in sinful eating habits or an obsession with exercise. The ripple effects of this falsehood can leave a wake of misery.

The good news is that Jesus provides a glorious solution to this slander. Jesus takes this one head-on and offers truth that brings lasting joy. Jesus, the most important person in human history, had no physical beauty that would have drawn us to him. Isaiah 53:2–3 says,

> For he grew up before him like a young plant,
>   and like a root out of dry ground;
> *he had no form or majesty that we should look at him,*
>   *and no beauty that we should desire him.*
> He was despised and rejected by men,

>   a man of sorrows and acquainted with grief;
>   and as one from whom men hide their faces
>   he was despised, and we esteemed him not.

Jesus was despised and rejected by men in order to obtain salvation for the world. As believers, our identity and value is not in our "looks" but in our Christ.

The apostle Paul also reminds us that our inner self is more precious than our outer self that is wasting away (see 2 Cor. 4:16). Peter tells us not to let our adorning be external but to put on imperishable beauty (1 Peter 3:3–6). A gentle tone is better than a toned body. And a quiet spirit shows more than a slimmed stomach. In God's sight, the inner person is very precious. Beauty is in the eye of the beholder, and it is what the Creator finds beautiful that counts.

While it is important to keep up your physical appearance, developing inner character should be your primary focus. Next time Satan tempts you to dwell on your external appearance, remind yourself that you are created in the image of God and are being conformed into the glorious image of Christ (Rom. 8:29). Remind yourself that you are pursuing holiness, which is worth more than a thousand rubies.

The good news is that Jesus never forsakes his children nor has the final "we need to talk" conversation. The steadfast love of the Lord never fails. He can be trusted the moment before a relationship begins and the moment after a relationship ends. Spend your days at his feet instead of at the mirror. As you continue to look into Christ's radiant face, your face will glow with his glory (see 2 Cor. 3:18).

Until then,
Sean and Jenny

DISCUSSION QUESTIONS

1. Which lies are you most tempted to believe?
2. What are two truths from Scripture that can combat those lies?
3. Are there any areas in your spiritual walk that need attention? If so, what are a few steps you can take to grow in these areas?

SHOULD I GUARD MY HEART?

Spencer

Dear Romantic,

Your well-meaning friend just told you, "Be sure to guard your heart!" You have been told to build at least two boundaries in your relationship: physical purity and emotional caution. While guarding your body so that you can give it away later within the covenant of marriage makes sense, the reasoning for emotional caution can be unclear.

WHY SHOULD WE GUARD OUR HEARTS?

Typically, the reasons we have for guarding the heart have to do with consequences, not causes. You don't want your relationship to end with your heart still tied to another person. Emotional vulnerability goes hand in hand with physical intimacy, and you want to avoid temptation. You don't want to fog your ability to assess a relationship objectively by giving over too much of yourself.

These consecuences certainly help us to see the adverse effects of not guarding our hearts. But these still are not reasons or purposes for establishing emotional boundaries in our lives. So why should we guard our hearts, and how do we do it?

THE SOURCE OF LIFE

Most conversations about guarding the heart before marriage start with Proverbs 4:23: "Keep your heart with all vigilance, for from it flow the springs of life." Your heart is important in the same way that a water source is important to a city. Without water, the city will wither and die; therefore, the city guards its water supply with vigilance.

Our hearts are important because they indicate *who we really are.* Your heart is composed of your deepest affections, desires, and motivations. The Bible teaches that people murder, commit adultery, and steal not primarily because of their circumstances or upbringing but because of their *hearts* (see Matt. 15:19). More importantly, the Bible teaches that Christians can actually do good in the world because they have a *new heart* (see Ezek. 36:26–27; Rom. 6:17). Your heart is important because it is a worship center that reveals your God. Your heart is also important because it is fragile. The reason why the New Testament always calls us as Christians to renew our minds (see Rom. 12:2) and set our minds on things above (see Col. 3:2) is because our hearts are prone to wander. Recognizing the fragility of your heart allows you to see the need for vigilance.

If this is true, then guarding your heart really means guarding your worship. Guarding your heart is important primarily because God is important. If we guard our hearts out of a motivation for self-protection, suspicion, or pride, we miss the point entirely. We guard our hearts because we are seeking to worship

God alone. Worship puts everything else—including a romantic relationship—in its proper place. Roots before fruits.

GUARDING THROUGH WORSHIP

Heart guarding is marked by worship of our great God and by self-forgetful love of others. Heart guarding is not an overly suspicious view of people or yourself that is constantly wringing its hands and wondering if it has given too much of itself away. Guarding your heart is about normal Christian living, not about obsessing over your romantic relationship. This demystifies the process of guarding your heart and gives you and your significant other a clear way to discern whether your relationship is in its proper place. Consider these two categories with your partner:

Do we delight in the person of Jesus Christ? Our preferences, the way we spend our time, and our thoughts often show us what we care about most. In dating, engagement, and marriage, we are called not just to pursue a relationship with another person but to pursue a relationship with the living Christ. If your love for Christ has decreased, don't despair—repent. If you spend time with your partner but neglect time reading the Bible and praying, resolve not to spend time together until you have been alone with God. We grow in our love for Christ by beholding him in his Word. Confess your sins and ask another Christian to help you walk by the Spirit.

Do we lay our lives bare before other Christians? You cannot guard a castle with only one guard. When was the last time someone spoke with you about your soul? If you and your partner are consistently isolating yourselves, your hearts are probably tied up in each other, not in Christ (see Prov. 18:1). If you cannot name another Christian who has asked you an uncomfortable question in the last few months, don't despair—turn and move toward living in biblical community. Initiate a conversation with another Christian this week about your Christian life.

GUARDING AS A WAY OF LIFE

Guarding your heart is not just important for dating. Guarding your heart is important for your wedding day, marriage, and the day you say goodbye to your spouse at death. As you pursue this relationship with your partner, you are building the foundations of your future relationship. Now is the time to build together a foundation of love for Christ. Not only will this encourage the right kind of love for each other, it will also allow you to care for your partner without suspicion. This is a love that sees your partner not as your god but as a fellow heir of grace; not as your everything but as your partner in the fight of faith.

Guard your heart by guarding your worship. Cultivate habits of worshiping God alone together. This heart of worship results in two people who are naked and unashamed (see Gen. 2:25) relating to each other without shame or distrust because they worship God in spirit and in truth. As we grow in our love for Christ and in the worship of God, God slowly fulfills his mission to restore and return us—and our relationships—to the garden.

Until then,
Spencer

DISCUSSION QUESTIONS

1. Do you love Jesus more than your partner? Why or why not?
2. How do you define "guarding your heart" biblically?
3. On a scale of 1 to 10, how open are you with older Christians in your life? If you gave yourself a low score on the scale, how can you become more transparent with others?

SEXUAL HISTORY

Spencer

Dear Romantic,

Things are getting more serious between you and your partner. You see growth in your affections toward one another. Trusted friends affirm your relationship. Both of you are growing in Christlikeness. This is a sweet and important season, and you are now beginning to consider deep and important aspects of your relationship.

It is important to talk with your partner about each of your pasts. Although our identities are not wrapped up in our past, our history often colors the way that we view the world and influences the way we think about relationships. Because of this, it's important to communicate about any past sexual sins in both your life and theirs.

From conversations you have had with each other over the last few months, you realize that your partner is not a virgin. You have danced around the topic a few times before, but it's time to talk about it. It's good to have this discussion during this season of your relationship, but before you do, I think it would benefit you to give some forethought to this conversation.

FEEL THE RESPONSIBILITY

When you ask your partner to share this aspect of their past, you are asking them to give you a piece of their heart. Sexual sin is deeply painful and makes up the most vulnerable part of a person's story. You should tremble as you consider being entrusted with this part of your partner's story. This is not information to be learned; it is a responsibility for you to steward. Are you ready for this stewardship?

Remember, your partner does not automatically owe this information to you. One way to know if you are ready for this stewardship is to evaluate whether you are on a trajectory toward marriage. If you are going to ask for this piece of their heart, you should do so in the context of commitment. This does not mean waiting until after you are engaged to have this conversation. However, you should be serious and be moving toward the promise of marriage. This should be one of many conversations that you have as you consider whether God is leading you to covenant together.

A CROSS-SHAPED TONE

Your partner is not sharing their past sin with you as a form of penance. It's tempting to listen to the pestering voice of Satan and the lies of condemnation he whispers into our ears when we retell our stories. You must silence the lies of Satan with the verdict of Christ's cross. Jesus has paid for your partner's sins, forgiven them, and declared them clean (see Rom. 8:1; 1 Cor. 6:9–11). No one can condemn your partner, because God's justifying voice drowns out all other voices (see Rom. 8:33–34). The story that your partner shares with you is simply the road to Zion.

Your tone should take the shape of the cross. Do not demand to hear every detail of their story or the frequency of their sin. What's most important for you to know is the reality of the sin and the ways in which it may still affect you and your partner.

RESPONDING TO THE NEW PERSON

Convictions are tested and refined when they grate against the sharp edges of this fallen world. I'm sure you have already considered how you will respond to this conversation. You may be concerned that it will be too much for you to handle. But as you prepare yourself for this conversation you must not mistake who your partner *was* for who they *are* now. Your partner is not someone who has a "rough past" but rather an individual whose past has been swallowed up in the death of Christ. You are called to respond to who your partner is in Christ. The Holy Spirit has given your partner new life, united them to Christ, and indwelt them as a child of God (see Rom. 8:15–17). As you go into this conversation, commit to respond to who your partner *is* as you hear about who they *were*.

There is, however, still space for you to process the different pieces of your partner's story. Although past sexual sin is forgiven by Christ, and although you see your partner as a new creation in Christ, you may have questions that you want to ask. For some people, past sexual sin makes the idea of sex within marriage a scary reality. For other people, there may be physical ramifications to their past lifestyle that need to be discussed. Although there is no formula for timing, I would recommend having these conversations *before* engagement so that you have ample time to listen, understand, and adjust your relationship at your own pace.

Sorting through the ramifications of past sin can be emotional and difficult. Before you have this conversation, I would recommend asking an older Christian couple to be present for it. They will be able to give perspective and clarity as you work through these complex issues.

DO NOT CALL DIRTY WHAT CHRIST HAS CALLED CLEAN

Some relationships sever over these complexities. One person is unable to reconcile their partner's past with their own path, and the couple painfully parts ways. I believe this is a tragic mistake and would encourage you not to end your relationship just because your partner is not a virgin (unless of course there are continuing effects, such as hidden or ongoing sin). Soak your expectations in the biblical picture of the new birth. Do not call dirty what God has called clean.

I still remember sitting on the couch with my future wife as she shared the story of her past sexual sin. The quietness of the room was broken by her tears as she shared her story. These were confident tears that knew the forgiving gaze of her God, but she still felt the pang of sin. This was a night of long conversations as well as many questions and answers. Yet, as we worked through these issues together, we grew closer to each other and more confident in the power of the Holy Spirit. Jesus really does change us and make us new. My wife wore white on her wedding day to reflect her purity before God and man—I pray that you and your partner will begin to see each other as pure in Christ regardless of your sexual history.

Though your sins are like scarlet,
they shall be as white as snow;
though they are red like crimson,
they shall become like wool.
—Isaiah 1:18

Until then,
Spencer

DISCUSSION QUESTIONS

1. What aspects of having this conversation make you most nervous?
2. What particular details from your partner's past do you think are essential to know? Share these with a pastor and mentor.

WHAT IF I'M NOT A VIRGIN?

Spencer and Taylor

Dear Romantic,

Dread.

This can often be the first feeling when you consider sharing your sexual history with your partner. Even after repentance, lingering "what ifs" still remain. What if I bring baggage into the relationship? What if we get married and I struggle to be intimate with my spouse? What if I have a worldly perspective on sex? What if I bring my spouse down? What if we can't have children? The unknowns surrounding the conversation can paralyze you with fear. How do you explain your past?[1]

---

1. This chapter is specifically meant to help those who are seeking to explain past sexual sin for which they are responsible. It is not meant to address the complexities that arise from a partner explaining a story of abuse or rape.

For helpful resources with navigating issues related to rape and abuse, see Pamela Gannon and Beverly Moore, *In the Aftermath: Past the Pain of Childhood Sexual Abuse* (Bemidji, MN: Focus Publishing, 2017), and David Powlison, *Recovering from Child Abuse: Healing and Hope for Victims* (Greensboro, NC: New Growth Press, 2008).

The burden you feel makes sense. This is likely one of the hardest conversations you will have with your partner as you progress in your relationship. You are stepping into vulnerable territory as you share some of the most tender parts of your story. These are delicate details that must be handled with care.

But these delicate details are important to share because they are a glorious part of God's work in your life. They represent what God has done to make you who you are today. As you share your sexual history, you initiate a glorious introduction to a life that will be characterized by vulnerability and trust as you navigate through a fallen world. If you want to give yourself to your partner, this is a part of it. It's time to take this first step.

STRENGTH FOR TODAY, HOPE FOR TOMORROW

Sharing memories from past sexual sin can be like walking through a cemetery. While each memory is a gravestone of sin that has been put at the foot of Christ's cross, past sin can still have a deep effect on you today. As you recall your history, it can feel like your sins return to life, paralyzing you with doubt. Are you a fraud? Has Christ *really* changed you? Will your partner still want to be with you after you share all of this? These are the lies and accusations of the Devil—the accuser. He will accuse you as though you are still condemned for your sin, and he will try to persuade you that you are still who you were. These two tactics are his oldest tools.

Yet Satan's tools are not to be feared if you are hiding in Christ's forgiveness. As you prepare for this conversation, fill your mind with God's promises of forgiveness for his children. Although you may remember your past with crystal clarity, God does not (see Ps. 25:7). God promises his children that he has removed their sins from them "as far as the east is from the west"

(Ps. 103:12). Even if your partner were to treat you differently after this conversation, God will not (see Ps. 103:10). Because Christ was punished for your sexual history, God is faithful to forgive you (see 1 John 1:9). There is no anger toward you in God's mind. All of it was taken out on his Son. You can find strength in the promise of his forgiveness.

God's forgiveness in Christ means that you don't have to carry around your sexual sin like a scarlet letter. This is no longer who you are. God has declared you a new creation (see 2 Cor. 5:17)—so, although your feelings of dread might be real, they are not true. God has given you a new heart transformed by grace (see Ezek. 36:26). The details you are about to share with your partner can no longer identify you.

SHARING YOUR STORY

As you meditate on the truths of God's forgiveness, it is wise to consider *how* you will share the details of your sexual history. Here are four steps you can take to aid you as you think about sharing your story:

1. *Pray.* Pray over the truths of God's Word that are mentioned above. Ask him for faith and confess when you struggle to believe these truths. Thank God for his forgiveness of your past. Ask that these truths of God's forgiveness would comfort your partner as you share your sexual history.
2. *Invite a pastor or mentor.* Having a pastor or mentor present whom you are both familiar with, during this conversation, can help you to wade through the details of your story. Since this conversation can be emotional, it will help you to have a pastor or mentor available who is

not as personally involved in the relationship. This person can help you share and can help your partner understand by bringing clarity where there is confusion.

3. *Consider what you will share.* Before you meet with your partner, write down what you will share with them. Keep in mind that you should not share every detail of your sexual history. You need to tell them that you are not a virgin and need to communicate those details that have direct impact on them (STDs, fear of intimacy, abuse, and so on).

4. *Be patient.* You do not know how your partner will respond. Be patient with your partner as they listen, process, and ask questions. They may want to have follow-up conversations with you after they have had more time to think about your story and about making it part of their own.

As raw as this feels, this is loving to your partner. This brave step of sharing yourself with another is a testament to the gospel, which frees us to share our stories as trophies of grace. God is with you, he is for you, and he will continue to redeem and restore you until all things are made new.

Until then,
Spencer and Taylor

DISCUSSION QUESTIONS

1. How do you think your partner will respond to a conversation about your past sexual sin? What are you most nervous about?

2. As you prepare to share, pray through Psalm 131 and ask God to calm your heart.
3. Write out on a single page the main points of your story that you plan to share with your partner. You can give this to your mentor in advance in order to receive guidance.

WE JUST SINNED SEXUALLY

Sean

Dear Romantic,

Shame, fear, disappointment, and regret are emotions that often come after a couple has sinned together sexually. Perhaps you have just sinned in some way with your partner and are wondering what to do. Should you be concerned? Is it really that big of a deal? Should you take a break, break up, or continue to date?

THE PATH TO HEALING

As humans, our knee-jerk reaction is to run and cover up our sin. When Adam and Eve sinned in the garden of Eden and realized that they were naked, they hid from God. The very first act of sin in this world was followed by a cover-up attempt. Adam and Eve grasped for fig leaves to cover their shame, and they retreated back from the presence of God (see Gen. 3:7–8).

Perhaps you have sinned with your partner and are tempted to run away from the presence of Jesus. I want to encourage you to do the exact opposite.

The way to heal sexual sin is to run to Jesus as quickly as you can. God is a tender and gracious Father who is on the lookout for his children to repent (see Luke 15:20). Jesus did not come into the world to condemn the world but to save it (see John 3:17). I can guarantee this because Jesus bled on a wooden cross in order to forgive anyone who turns away from disobedience. Jesus will forgive all who believe that he is able to wipe away their sins.

God promises sweet relief for a troubled conscience in the book of Hebrews:

> Therefore, brothers, since we have confidence to enter the holy places by the blood of Jesus, by the new and living way that he opened for us through the curtain, that is, through his flesh, and since we have a great priest over the house of God, let us draw near with a true heart in full assurance of faith, with our hearts sprinkled clean from an evil conscience and our bodies washed with pure water. (Heb. 10:19–22)

Jesus takes dirty hearts and broken consciences and makes them clean and clear. There is nothing better than a clear conscience before God, and Jesus can give you forgiveness today if you ask him. There has never been a better time to enter into the presence of God. His arms are open wide, and the only thing keeping him from you is your pride and fear of judgment.

HOPE THROUGH HONESTY

The way to healing comes only through honesty. The Bible offers hope to everyone who walks in the light. If we do not walk in the light of truthfulness, we cannot have a relationship with God.

This is the message we have heard from him and proclaim to you, that God is light, and in him is no darkness at all. If we say we have fellowship with him while we walk in darkness, we lie and do not practice the truth. But if we walk in the light, as he is in the light, we have fellowship with one another, and the blood of Jesus his Son cleanses us from all sin. (1 John 1:5–7)

If you are unwilling to confess your sin to God and to mature Christians, then you are snuffing out all hope for healing. If you remain in the dark, sexual sin will become enslaving and will lead to death (see Rom. 6:23). It is so serious that God says that those who continue in sexual immorality will not enter the kingdom of heaven (see Rev. 21:8).

I specifically want to encourage you to avoid "technicalities" with your sin. "But sexual immorality and *all impurity* or covetousness must not even be named among you, as is proper among saints" (Eph. 5:3). The individual who wants to come clean is not concerned with whether or not they are a "technical virgin." The Pharisees, who were very good at parsing all the minutiae of sin, will be cast into the lake of fire, but the prostitutes, who wept and were broken at the feet of Jesus, will find life and peace.

Sexual sin will suffocate you unless you come completely clean. I have known couples who were willing to confess only part of their sin. They stated that they wanted to change, but they held on to aspects of their sin with clenched fists and did not give a full confession. If you are tempted to turn away from only half of your sin, you are still holding on to all of it.

THE PATH TO HOLINESS

All of this raises the question: "Should we end our relationship because we have sinned sexually together?" There are many factors that play into answering this, but these questions need to be addressed first: "How often has this sin occurred?" "Is this sin an isolated incident, a pattern, or a mixture of both?"

Patterns of sin often reveal hearts that are not in love with Jesus. If you are noticing sexual sin in your relationship together, now is the time to seek out a mentor and give attention to your personal walk with Christ. Though it can be painful, ending a romantic relationship that is fueling sexual sin is the best course of action. If you are habitually falling into sin, breaking up will allow you to focus on pursuing holiness before romance. There is nothing more important than knowing the presence of Christ (see Ps. 27:4).

If this sexual sin was a one-time event for you, you need to know that sexual activity does not randomly take place. By the time someone commits a physical sexual sin, there have been numerous transgressions committed at the heart level. All physical acts of sin come from the heart.

After confession of sin has taken place, you must chart an intentional path away from that disobedience. This change must occur in your heart, head, and hands. It is best to reach out to a wise, godly couple for assistance in making a plan for change.

When charting a new course toward purity, you need to take the following steps:

- Confess to a spiritual authority. It is best if this is someone who can hold you accountable and offer you mature advice.
- Clear boundaries must be reestablished. Jesus talks about being radical in your efforts to fight against sin and temptation. In Matthew 5:29–30, he mentions cutting off hands and plucking out eyes in order to attack sin. Apply this to your situation. What were the circumstances around the sin? Why did it happen? Were you alone and in a

compromising situation? How can you "cut off a hand" or "pluck out an eye" to prevent it from happening again?

- Evaluate your entire relationship. Are you both at a spiritually mature enough level to consider pursuing marriage? Are you ready to love and protect each other by setting the bar of purity higher? Do you both want to honor God more than to enjoy the fleeting pleasures of sin?

This moment of failure can become a moment of victory. This sin may be the very act that God uses to get your attention and refocus your life on holiness. Jesus loves to take our weaknesses and make us strong. Let us pray for grace to make us pure in heart and hands in order that we might see God.

Until then,
Sean

DISCUSSION QUESTIONS

1. Are there any sins you are hiding? If you are tempted to cover up your sin instead of confessing it, take a moment to meditate on Proverbs 28:13 and 1 John 1:9.
2. What were your thoughts and desires before and after you sinned with your partner?
3. Would you and your partner benefit from spending time exclusively focused on the Lord instead of pursuing each other romantically?
4. Work with a mentor to write down four ways you can prevent sexual sin from occurring again in the future.

ON KISSING

Sean

Dear Romantic,

For couples who want to honor Christ and each other, discussing and deciding on physical boundaries is essential. Many people want to know where to draw the line sexually. At one time in my life, I wanted to know how close I could get to "the line" without crossing it. It took me a while to realize that I was asking the wrong question. I should have been asking, "How can I honor the Lord and love my significant other in purity?"

One question that Jenny and I wrestled with in our relationship was whether or not we should kiss. There was no question in our minds about whether we *wanted* to kiss or not. That was settled: we were eager. Yet we both wanted to make an informed decision about our physical affection and not be too hasty. To make a long story short, we came to believe that kissing (as well as all romantic physical affection) should be saved exclusively for marriage.

We suggest refraining from kissing until you say your vows. Our philosophy on the subject might seem radical, but let that be attractive rather than repelling. Just because something initially seems "extreme" does not mean that it should be easily dismissed. If that were the case, we could dismiss almost everything that Jesus said (see Matt. 7:14). Let me try to convince you briefly why I believe it is most honoring to God to save physical affection for marriage. Some of the reasons below are rooted in biblical texts, while others are more anecdotal.

First, romantic kissing shows commitment. Kisses communicate. At minimum, a kiss is supposed to be a special sign of deep friendship. Consider Psalm 2:12: "Kiss the Son, lest he be angry." This passage communicates what everyone knows deep down: a kiss is not "just a kiss." In this text, Jesus wants exclusive devotion, submission, and love, all of which are symbolized by the imagery of a kiss. Kissing communicates *something*. This is what makes a "holy kiss" holy (see Rom. 16:16) and Judas's betrayal so wicked (see Luke 22:48). If kissing communicated nothing, then no one would care about it. Since kisses communicate, a romantic kiss is sexual in a way that other kisses are not, conveying special covenantal language that is designed to be cherished exclusively in marriage.

Second, you are dating your brother or sister—not your spouse. A spouse is a companion, friend, spiritual sibling, and partner in the gospel of grace. The difference between a spouse and a girlfriend is not fundamentally on the spiritual level but on the sexual level. The only romantic physical affection that is shown in Scripture is between a man and woman in marriage. We are called to treat our sisters with absolute purity (see 1 Tim. 5:2).

Third, we want to do everything possible to present our brides to ourselves in splendor, without any spot or wrinkle or blemish (see Eph. 5:27). Not one wrinkle, not even a single blemish on the garment of purity, should be found. Refraining from kissing will help you accomplish this and lessen the pressure of temptation. We should be eager to hold the bar of purity high for the sake of Christ. These matters must be carefully thought out, because we will all stand before God and give an account of our relationships. Jesus was committed to the self-sacrifice of a rugged cross in order to obtain our purity. How far are you willing to go in order to present to yourself a spotless bride?

Fourth, kissing is like jumping out of an airplane. It starts the thrill of skydiving. You can pull a parachute, but once you've started the descent, it's very hard to turn back. To begin and then stop halfway every time goes against the laws of gravity. I know countless couples who started with kissing but then proceeded into more intense territory. If you are pursuing purity, why even go down this road? God calls us to flee temptation instead of revving its engine (see 1 Cor. 6:18).

Fifth, why not maximize your pleasure? Personally, I am the kind of guy who thinks it is exciting to save dessert for last. The same applies here. It is also hard to forget the face of one of my best friends (who happens to be Spencer) when he kissed his bride for the first time. He was beside himself. The moment was electric, and they were ecstatic. There is something exciting about a bride and groom kissing those long-awaited lips.

Sixth, no matter how promising it looks, you are simply not guaranteed marriage until you say your vows. Until then, it is a kind and loving act to make sure that you are not kissing someone else's bride or groom. Don't be afraid to love your significant other by saving kissing for marriage. Your partner will respect you all the more for your decision (1 Thess. 4:4–7).

I remember once when Jenny and I were talking with a girl in our living room about physical affection. She had been involved with many boyfriends, and kissing had been a part of all her relationships. She inquired about our dating relationship and was shocked to find that we had saved kissing for our wedding day.

She wanted kissing to be unique to her future husband, but it had become common. I say this because she had not intended to break up with any of the guys she had dated. She had entered into relationships thinking they were going to last and hoping that every boyfriend was the final one. In each relationship, she had good intentions of staying together. If she had started out intentionally refraining from romantic physical affection with her first boyfriend, it would have kept her from this heartache. We had the privilege of telling her that it wasn't too late to redeem this gift and that God specializes in making things new (see Joel 2:25; 2 Cor. 5:17). This leads to the final reason.

Seventh, I've never met anyone who regretted this decision. However, I've met many couples who wish they had saved more for their marriage. I kissed my first girlfriend in middle school, and I wish I could take it back a thousand times over. Not because it was an unpleasant experience, but because I could have honored her and my future spouse. I could have reserved that experience for the true love of my life.

I lay these things before you for your consideration. Jenny and I both kissed others in previous relationships but then decided to refrain from kissing each other until marriage. It was a struggle at times to refrain from physical affection, but it was worth every ounce of self-control.

I have tried to give you compelling reasons to refrain from kissing until marriage, but I have not given you a chapter and verse that says, "Thou shall not touch lips." It is not my goal to argue that it is impossible to be godly and kiss before marriage. My goal is to encourage you to make an informed decision based on Scripture, be intentional to honor your future spouse, and pursue purity with a heart of love. If you find yourself agreeing with me, please do not make these things a law for others. Instead, be convinced in your own mind and humbly take pleasure in purity for the glory of Christ. In your decision, remember that the most important matter is a pure heart (see Matt. 5:8). You can still sin sexually even though you technically "have never kissed." It would be tragic for you to draw near to Jesus with your lips but to have your heart be far from him (see Matt. 15:8).

Until then,
Sean

DISCUSSION QUESTIONS

1. What are the physical boundaries in your romantic relationship? Be specific.
2. Do you and your partner agree on the physical parameters you have established? Why or why not?
3. What are the biblical reasons behind the boundaries you have established?
4. In what ways are you cultivating purity of heart in addition to physical purity?

EXPRESSING YOUR LOVE

Spencer

Dear Romantic,

Dating is a complicated dance—especially when you are trying to avoid sin.

Dating as a Christian pulls you in two opposite directions. First, you experience the tug of affection for your partner. You spend more time together, and your heart swells with warmth and care. You rejoice in the presence of your partner and, naturally, desire to express that joy. In addition, because God created you as an embodied person, you usually express your emotions physically: you hug the people you love, cry over losses, and sometimes even jump with joy. You have a body. You were made for this.

Enter the second (and opposite) tug.

Although your heart swells with love and you desire to show this love physically, you also feel the tug of biblical truth. Even though God gave you a body, he wants you to control it (see 1 Thess. 4:4). He didn't make it for sexual immorality (see 1 Cor. 6:13). Instead, he commands you to flee immorality at all costs (see 1 Cor. 6:18) and wants you to keep the marriage bed undefiled (Heb. 13:4). Although you feel the pull to express your affection physically, God's Word tugs you in the opposite direction.

You and your partner live within the tension of these seemingly opposing desires. To add to the confusion, when some of your friends talk about affection during dating, they typically talk about it in negative terms. "Don't be alone in the car." "Don't kiss each other." "Don't touch each other there." Although these specific prohibitions are important, they are not the full story.

Outside of knowing what *not* to do, is there a way forward? How do you kindle appropriate affection in your relationship while honoring God with your body?

TRANSFORM HOW YOU THINK ABOUT BOUNDARIES

The temptation of the serpent in the garden worked because Satan blurred the *purpose* of boundaries. Why were they not allowed to eat of the tree in the garden? Satan said it was because God didn't want them to grow in knowledge and was holding things back from them (see Gen. 3:5). The first couple was convinced by the serpent that their God-given boundaries were not intended for life (see Gen. 2:17), so they broke them. This insidious lie took root in their hearts, and the curse with its consequences pulsated through the world.

What is your response to God's righteous boundaries? Are they a pointless burden meant to keep you in line? Or are they lamps that light the path to life? More specifically, what do you think about the boundaries of *your relationship*? Satan wants us to believe that God's commandments are burdensome (see 1 John 5:3). This is that ancient lie of the serpent that plunged our race into the dark waters of the curse.

Expressing Your Love

The best way to combat the lie of the serpent is to renew your mind with God's good purposes for your relationship. When you discuss boundaries with your partner, talk about them as a means to store up pleasure rather than as a temporary misery that must be endured. Do not say, "We can't do this together because the Bible says we can't." Instead, say this: "We choose to save this to be enjoyed within the covenant of marriage."

To be sure, the call to purity can be difficult. However, comfort and joy are found when we view our difficulties through the lens of God's good purposes and promises for us as his children. This starts in your heart. Meditate on the goodness of God's purpose for boundaries. You're storing up pleasure for later. Very soon, you will experience God's good gifts in God's good time under God's good smile. Transform your thinking.

PATTERNS BECOME PERMANENT

Although intimacy is a vital part of marriage, it is a relatively small part when compared to the various aspects of your relationship with your spouse. Much of marriage happens outside of the marriage bed. So during this time, when the fruit of marriage is forbidden, explore the other trees in the garden. The memories you make now, the habits you cultivate, the relationships you pursue—all of these things are patterns that will affect the fragrance of your marriage.

Some couples miss the wonderful "yeses" of this season of life because they are so focused on the "nos" of their relationship. When you are convinced that the only way to show affection is through physical intimacy, you miss the potential for love in other areas of life: taking long walks, setting out on road trips, serving saints in your church, eating with friends, adventuring in your city, and asking questions. These habits of pursuing each

123

other outside the marriage bed will become patterns in your relationship. Furthermore, they will serve to bind your hearts together through shared experiences and memories. Make patterns now while you wait for intimacy.

TRUST THE DIVINE SEQUENCE

In fact, the patterns you create while waiting for intimacy will actually improve your marital intimacy. The joy of the bride and groom in the Song of Solomon is a symphony of emotional, relational, and physical delight. They experience the security of belonging (see Song 6:3), the joy of friendship (see Song 5:16), and the intensity of physical intimacy (see Song 4). The poem is composed of all these elements. This is the divine sequence.

It makes more sense to touch each other's hearts before you touch each other's bodies.[1] The sweetness of the wedding night—the reason why they call it *consummation*—comes as the rightful climax to a million shared moments, memories, joys, sorrows, conversations, experiences, and adventures. And when you do finally touch each other, you will find that you are participating in a divine sequence—one that compounds your joy and intensifies your pleasure.

DEEP ROOTS

In this season of pursuing the heart rather than touching the body, you are nurturing deep roots. If God blesses your relationship with marriage, you will discover that friendship and intimacy are woven together. The cultivation of friendship

---

1. See C. J. Mahaney, *Sex, Romance, and the Glory of God* (Wheaton, IL: Crossway, 2004), chap. 3.

solidifies the foundation of marriage. So don't lose sight of the beauty of the garden because you are obsessed with the forbidden tree. Explore, cultivate, and find adventure in the current stage you are in. Soon you will find that the exploration never ends.

Until then,
Spencer

DISCUSSION QUESTIONS

1. What habits can you cultivate now that you would like to see in your marriage?
2. Are any of God's righteous boundaries hard for you to accept? Which ones? Why?
3. What are some ways you can cultivate love with your partner that honor God and each other?

AM I TOO YOUNG
FOR MARRIAGE?

Sean

Dear Romantic,

How young is too young to get married? When Jenny and I started contemplating marriage, I looked much younger than twenty years old. People wondered whether I could even shave, let alone start a family (and many people still think this). When someone expresses a desire for early marriage, the murmurs among relatives can rumble, and friends may even prophesy doom.

And it might just be that their concerns are warranted. After all, divorce rates are high, and they don't want you to follow suit. I've always wondered whether statistics on divorce included early marriages. If so, these figures must come from recent polls, because if they included everyone's grandparents, surely that would tip the scales in a positive direction. My grandparents got married at nineteen and twenty-one years old and just celebrated their seventy-fifth anniversary.

Regardless, all the concerns about early marriage might be 100 percent valid if you are driven by lust and live in your parents' basement. If that is the case, we should all bar the chapel doors from you. So the question must be asked: what qualifies you to get married at such an early age?

Here are some guidelines to think about as you consider this question.

SPIRITUALLY

Is your walk with Jesus thriving and growing? The book of Psalms says that the Word makes you wiser than all your teachers (see Ps. 119:99). God is not a respecter of age. His Spirit can quicken the young and mature them at lightning speed. The Scriptures do not card you before they give you bottles of strong wisdom.

As a man, do you feel comfortable standing before God and being held responsible for the spiritual direction of your wife? Adam was responsible for the spiritual direction of Eve. Don't think that God will let you slide by easy. As a woman, are you growing in your walk with Christ? Are you ready to serve your family? Raising a family is a serious calling, and we should be prepared and sober-minded before we answer.

FINANCIALLY

Are you as a man able to support a family? As a woman, are you marrying someone who is a hard worker and able to secure a job? It is not sexy to buy each other flowers and chocolates with money borrowed from parents. If you cannot provide for your household, you are worse than an unbeliever (see 1 Tim. 5:8). You must literally count the cost before you get married. It is a good idea to plan and present your budget to your parents or a trusted mentor.

But neither should you buy the lie of the American dream. You can live on much less than what most people in our culture think it takes. You don't need to have thousands of dollars in the bank beforehand; you don't have to eat out twice a week; you don't have to live on prime real estate; you don't need to have new furniture or two well-tuned cars. You need food for energy and clothing for when you leave the apartment (see 1 Tim. 6:8).

DIRECTIONALLY

You need to have a God-honoring trajectory. You need to be gripped by the gospel and driven for the glory of God. You don't have to have all the details worked out, but you do need a direction. Before you get hitched, you should have an idea about the general direction you are pursuing for your life.

Will you finish college?

If so, how will this happen?

Will you be living in a new location?

Will you be pursuing a particular job?

Will your partner be in school?

When do you want children?

These are not softball questions to toss around in the backyard. Wise counsel must be loaded into these conversations as you prepare a cannon for firing. Each of these questions involves a lot of detail, but the main issue is that you must find your passion in life. What makes you surge for the glory of God? Life is too precious and God is too glorious for us to waste our lives. There are souls at stake and disciples to make. John Piper says it well.

> The people that make a durable difference in the world are not the people who have mastered many things, but who have been mastered by one great thing. If you want your life to count, if you want the ripple effect of the pebbles you drop to become waves that reach the ends of the earth and roll on into eternity, you don't need to have a high IQ. You don't have to have good looks or riches or come from a fine family or a fine school. Instead you have to know a few great, majestic, unchanging, obvious, simple, glorious things—or one great all-embracing thing—and be set on fire by them.[1]

You might not come from a rich family or a fine school, but these things don't determine the purpose of life. Are you captivated by a "few great things" that count for eternity? Are you "set on fire" for God's fame? This is the most important question when it comes to marriage.

So should you get married young?

If you are unprepared spiritually, financially, or directionally, the answer is no. But I do not think that marriage should be postponed because of a numerical value. Scripture says to "rejoice in the wife of your youth" (Prov. 5:18) and that a marriage partner is a good gift (see 1 Cor. 7:7). God gave us passions so that we can pursue them in biblically mature, God-honoring ways. Do not let anyone look down on you because you are young, as long as you are setting the standard in faith, life, love, and purity (see 1 Tim. 4:12).

Until then,
Sean

1. John Piper, *Don't Waste Your Life* (Wheaton, IL: Crossway, 2003), 44.

DISCUSSION QUESTIONS

1. Do you feel ready to pursue marriage? Why or why not?
2. If not, what are three practical steps you can take in order to begin preparing for marriage?
3. What is your all-consuming passion in life? Write it out in one paragraph.

CONCLUSION

THE BRIDGE (NEXT STEPS)

Sean and Spencer

Dear Romantic,

You have been dating for a while, and now the time has come to consider moving forward. The sun of dating is setting, and the dawn of engagement is rising. What should you do next?

We have previously written about the significance of the local church in the decisions you make about romance. The blessing and importance of godly community cannot be overstated. "Without counsel plans fail, but with many advisers they succeed" (Prov. 15:22). "Where there is no guidance, a people falls, but in an abundance of counselors there is safety" (Prov. 11:14).

The next step you should take toward engagement is actually not one that involves your partner. Rather, it involves those who know you and your partner best. It is essential for you to get counsel from others and to place yourselves outside any personal echo chambers. If you haven't done so already, now is the time to consider the following questions:

- Do your pastors or older mentors think it is a good idea for you to take the next steps toward marriage?
- Have you spoken to your partner's parents about your desire to pursue marriage and asked for their evaluation of your relationship?
- Are you and your partner the only ones who think your plan to get engaged is a good idea?

There are many churches that offer pre-engagement counseling. If this route is available, take full advantage of it. The church is designed to build one another up, bear one another's burdens, and help you to cross the bridge to engagement and marriage (see Eccl. 4:12; Gal. 6:2; 1 Thess. 5:11).

There are many other questions you need to discuss as you pursue engagement. These questions will include everything from the length of your engagement to preparations for your wedding night. We are eager to continue writing to you in *Letters to a Romantic: On Engagement* as you enter this exciting season. We pray that God will continue to grow both you and your partner as you behold the glory of the Lord and are daily transformed into his image through his Word (see 2 Cor. 3:18). Few things bring us more joy than to know that you are walking in the truth (see 3 John 4).

Until then,
Sean and Spencer

ACKNOWLEDGMENTS

This book would not have been possible without the assistance of others. Numerous pastors, friends, and family members have contributed to this project in ways that they don't even realize. Our parents have supported us throughout this endeavor—not to mention throughout our entire lives.

Many of our thoughts and ideas have come from other people, and we are especially indebted to godly mentors like Heath Lambert and Gunner Gundersen. Sean has deep gratitude for the Association of Biblical Counselors for endorsing this work. The staff and board at ACBC have been instrumental, essential, and gracious throughout the whole process. Spencer would also like to thank the leaders of Immanuel Baptist Church for their influence in his life and the precious saints at Vine Baptist Church for their constant support and encouragement.

We especially want to thank those who read the manuscript in advance and provided valuable feedback. Some of those people include Ben and Naomi Fennell, Nate and Jana Grote, Brad Taunton, Brennan Kolbe, Renee Hoskins, Ruth Anne Irvin, Cheri Evenson, Amy Evenson, Kayla Godbold, Kaity Glick, Samantha Crick, and Amanda Martin. A special thanks goes to Ian Thompson for entertaining our thoughts and jump-starting this book.

Acknowledgments

Above all else, we want to thank our wives, who gave sacrificially in order to make this endeavor possible. They gave priceless time and energy in order to bring this project to fruition. Their love, wisdom, and sacrifice are irreplaceable and have not gone unnoticed.

We are truly humbled by our Lord Jesus. We are grateful to God for every good and perfect gift he has given to us through others and from above. We are so thankful that he has spoken through his Word and that the Word became flesh. This book is just one attempt to sit beside the sufficient and glorious streams of Scripture and learn from them.

Sean Perron graduated with his MDiv from The Southern Baptist Theological Seminary and is currently chief of staff at the Association of Certified Biblical Counselors (ACBC). He and his wife Jennifer live in Jacksonville, Florida.

Spencer Harmon is pastor at Vine Street Baptist Church in Louisville, Kentucky. He and his wife Taylor have two daughters.

Together Sean and Spencer write on their website: www.unspokenblog.org.

Association of Certified
Biblical Counselors

Since 1976, the Association of Certified Biblical Counselors (ACBC) has been training and certifying biblical counselors to ensure excellence in the counseling room by faithfulness to the Word of God. We offer a comprehensive biblical counseling certification program that is rigorous, but attainable by even the busiest pastor or church member. Our certification process is made up of three phases: learning, exams and application, and supervision.

ACBC has grown from a handful of individuals to thousands of certified counselors all around the world. Now in our fourth decade of pursuing excellence in biblical counseling, we have had five executive directors: Dr. Bob Smith, Dr. Howard Eyrich, Rev. Bill Goode, and Rev. Randy Patten. Dr. Heath Lambert became the fifth executive director in 2013.

Every Christian is called to speak the truth in love to one another. ACBC trains Christians in their gospel responsibility to be disciple-makers and to build up the body of Christ. This training is accomplished through conferences and events throughout the world.

For more information about ACBC and biblical counseling resources, visit www.biblicalcounseling.com.